EMPATH

The Ultimate Guide to Master Your Gift, Overcome Fears, Manage Yourself and Use Your Potential to Get Your Personal Freedom.

By Victor Murphy

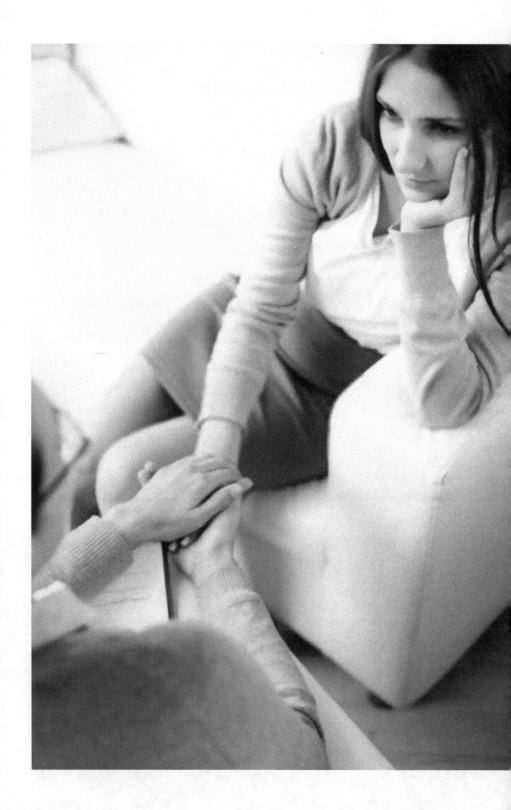

Copyright © 2021 by Victor Murphy

Legal Disclaimer

Table of Contents

Introduction

You walk into your office one morning and there is a strange person standing near the windows. Is she a client? A new member of the staff? You realize it doesn't matter as what matters is the pain flowing off of her like lava from a volcano.

You're going to your best friend's a 21st-anniversary party but there's this feeling of doom that you just can't shake. You really don't even want to go. What's wrong has nothing to do with you. At the end of the evening, your friends announce that they are getting a divorce.

You enter your parents' home for Thanksgiving dinner and find the house is just radiating with joy – overflowing with excitement. Yet no one is saying anything to explain this. No one else even seems to notice. Once you sit down to dinner your brother announces that he is getting married.

Are you an empath? Do you know things about others that you cannot know? Do you "sense" things that others do not? Can you feel the presence of pain in another person even though they show no outward signs and have told you nothing?

If you answered yes to any of these questions, this book is for you.

If you see yourself in any of these scenarios, this book is for you.

If you think someone you care for might be an empath, this book is for you.

If you are simply curious about empaths, this book is for you.

In this book, we will look at the presence of empaths in our lives, our history, our culture. What is an empath? Is a person born an empath? Have there always been empaths throughout history or is it a new age phenomenon? Is it even real? How can empaths protect themselves from being overwhelmed by others feelings? Is your dog an empath?

These are all questions we will discuss throughout this book. We will help you to build the tools you need to be safe. We will help parents know what to do with children who are empaths. Being an empath can be an amazing experience and it can be a very painful and overwhelming one. We are here to help you learn to not only live with being an empath but to thrive. Understand that empaths can change the world for the better.

In the first few chapters, we will look at what it means to be an empath. Were you born that way or can it be learned? We will explore the presence of empaths throughout history and look at some famous individuals who were empaths. We will see what has been said about empaths through the ages.

Chapter four will deal with the new science – neurobiology – that is proving that empaths do exist. It is not a sham or a game. It's real and there is scientific data to back it up. What kind of studies have been done and what kind of evidence has been found to validate the empath?

Chapters five to seven will deal with living as an empath. What kind of potential do you have as an empath? What can you do? What is it like to grow up as an empath? Children face tremendous challenges growing up "normal" like everyone else. How does a child empath deal with all the additional feelings coming at him all the time and how you help them?

This is the business of chapter five is your potential and chapter seven looks at the spiritual tools available to you and how you can use them. Finally, we will talk about how to protect yourself from toxic people who want to consume you.

We will take a quick look at the question of animals being empaths. Is your dog one? We will close with a final chapter of celebrating your empathic gifts. What is the science surrounding this question? You might "know" your dog is an empath, but the animal behaviorist and the scientist might not agree. In this chapter, we look at the state of this science at this time and review many of the anecdotal pieces of evidence for empathic animals.

Celebrate how we are changing the world as we speak. Being an empath is a challenge. At the same time, there is a lot to celebrate. Did you know that the Cleveland Clinic has a CEO – a Chief Empathy Officer? Should more companies follow suit? What would a Chief Empathy Officer do?

Remember that to be an active empath is a gift. Celebrate the beautiful and joyful in the midst of the painful and often overwhelming. This book is our gift to help you on your way.

1 CHAPTER 1

What is an Empath?

Do you think you are an empath? Perhaps you *know* you are an empath. How do you explain that to others who might not understand or know what an empath is? Would you tell them that an empath is a person who can feel what another person is actually feeling without even being told? Would you say an empath is someone who vicariously picks up on what is going on with other people emotionally?

Those would be pretty good beginning explanations or definitions, but they would only tell a very small part of the story of what an empath is, what an empaths life is like, how empaths survive while feeling the emotions of those around them. If you are an empath and your friend is suffering from overwhelming grief, how do you deal with that grief overwhelming you? Being an empath is about energy and emotions. Not yours – but those of the people around you.

If you are an empath you can walk into a room full of people and "sense" that someone is hurting badly, or someone is very happy; someone else is scared and yet another person is hopeful and excited. You will "pick up" all these feelings and the energy that goes with them. It is the energy of the person who feels sad, happy, scared, excited that touches you and you feel what they feel. You feel the energy they are giving out.

Empathy and Sympathy

The word empathy – usually seen juxtaposed to sympathy – came into being in 1858 when it was first used and defined by Rudolf Lotze, the German philosopher. By empathy, he meant being aware of and actually experiencing the feelings of others without the other having shared all their feelings, experiences and thoughts with you.

When you sympathize with someone, they share with you their thoughts, experience, and feelings. You then respond comfortingly to them out of your own thoughts, experiences, and feelings about what they shared with you. Empathy does not require that they share all those things. The Empath just "picks up on it". The empath "just knows". Now, this may sound like voodoo or nonsense to you but in a later chapter, we will look at the scientific community's discovery and study of empathy and empaths.

There are very specific characteristics or traits of an empath. You can be highly "sensitive" to others and not be an empath. Only 2-3% of people are actually empaths, while 15-20% might be highly "sensitive". Of course, the empaths are in that 15-20%. A percentage that is growing with more interest in the activity, as it is something most of us can open ourselves up to more if we choose to do so. We may not become full-fledged empaths – but we may open to our already present but dormant "sensitivity".

The term empath is used incorrectly these days by many people who mistakenly label the highly sensitive person as an empath when they are not all the way there. It's possible they could be if they wanted to, but for now, they are not empaths. Here are the many traits, characteristics, experiences of a genuine empath.

Traits and Experiences That Tell You if You are an Empath

- Others People's Energy

Is that your own energy and emotion you are feeling or someone else's? You are not only touched by other's energy. You not only feel others' energy, but you also take it on and you take it into yourself. You take their energy and their emotions into yourself. When you are being sympathetic, the other person's energy and emotions stay external to your own. If you are being empathetic, you take them into yourself and you may not even know it.

Your energy field – and we all have one – begins to vibrate at the same frequency as the person whose feelings you are picking up. It can be so intense that if the other cries so do you. If they are angry, so are you. If you are not aware that you are an empath this will be very disconcerting. However, if you are an experienced empath you will know these are not your feelings. You will need a way to disperse this energy that is not yours. For the moment it is enough to know that that energy you are feeling is not yours.

- Intuition – Intuitive Ability

Empaths have intuition – no not everyone has it. The empath has intuition galore. As an empath, your intuition tells you what others are feeling. You know when you look at them, talk to them, and know what is happening with them without their every saying anything to you about it. Your "intuition" told you. It's almost as if you were inside the mind and heart of the other. You just know.

- The Empath's Energy is Easily Drained

Because you are always feeling the other's energy, yours gets drained. You are always using your energy in an attempt to heal or help the other person whose cares you can't escape. You are always taking on the emotions of others and their problems. There isn't a lot of energy left over for you. If you are giving and giving, with multiple people, or even if you are unable to shield yourself from those who are projected their cares, you will be drained easily.

When this happens, it is easy for the empath to get unbalanced; become angry or depressed. You might feel used or overwhelmed. If this is how you feel it is time to step back and take care of yourself. Learn to block other emotions. Remember you cannot save the world. You cannot help everyone. There is a time when you have to take care of yourself and renew your own energy.

- People with Problems are Attracted to the Empath

Not only does the empath pick up other people's energy and needs, but they also attract those same type of people to themselves. People who are broken are attracted to a healer. This is the situation with the empath and the person in pain. You are sending messages as much as you are receiving them. You are putting out a message that you are available to help. If you need a break stop putting out that message. Turn the message off. Ignore the people sending messages to you and they will stop sending them. If you are not open to help them, they won't be attracted to you. When you have had too much turn it off. Remember: you can't save the world.

- Empaths Struggle with Crowds

Knowing that an empath can "hear" or feel whatever anyone is projecting, makes it easy to understand how hard it might be to be in a crowd. Any crowd – on the streets, at a party, in a bar - any crowd and you can easily be on sensory overload. Imagine messages coming at you from every and all direction. You can't even sort them out – all these messages jumbled together.

As you walk down the street you pick up everyone's mood. You feel the energy they are sending out. If the energy is sad, it's sad energy you feel. If the energy is angry, it can feel like an assault. If the energy is overwhelming grief, it can send the empath to their knees. Without learning to shield, an extremely sensitive empath might not be able to even go to the grocery store.

- Where Can an Empath Live?

If the empath is this sensitive to the messages coming from everyone around them, their personal energy is constantly being drained. Where you live if you are an empath is important to your health. You need space and silence. Mental and emotional silence, not verbal silence. Without this space, the empath will be overwhelmed. You need a place to recharge, to renew, to get your energy refilled.

- Empaths are Extremely Sensitive to Other's Suffering

There is no way around it. This is one of the most common traits in empaths. You can't escape feeling what others are feeling. You suffer as they suffer. You cry as they cry. For some empaths, there are even physical symptoms of what others are feeling. They feel the same physical responses that the person sending the message feels. It's even possible for fake violence on television or in films to cause the same physical reaction in the empath. This is because they are so sensitive.

- The Empath Can See Through Others' Lies

It's hard for someone to lie to an empath. The empath knows they are lying. The empath is not clear about how she knows, but she knows. You have no proof they are lying, but you know they are. The good news is this trait of an empath helps you. It helps you know who you can trust and who you can't trust.

- The Empath is Gifted with the Ability to Heal Emotions of Others

The gift of the empath is to heal those who you have empathy for. Those you spend your time and energy with are the ones you are healing with your gift. This is why those who need to be healed are attracted to you.

13

You really listen because you really feel them and understand them within yourself. You're not thinking about what you are going to say next or what you are going to make for dinner. You are really listening to them and that is your gift. That gift will heal.

- Most empaths put everyone else ahead of themselves. The empath will solve everyone else's problems before they solve their own. It's easy for the empath to get so caught up in the problems of everyone they are feeling, that they lose themselves and their own issues. You must take time for yourself. You must heal yourself or rather give yourself time to heal. There will be times when you have no more to give. The time when you are totally drained by your giving out that you need to take time to for yourself.

Empaths are known to bury their own needs in order to answer everyone else's. You might not know you are suppressing your own issues. Still, you must learn how to take care of yourself. Don't push your own needs away. Empaths who take care of themselves won't burn out.

2 CHAPTER 2

Nature or Nurture?

So, are empaths born or taught? Can you learn to be an empath? Are psychic empaths different from any other empath or are they all the same? There isn't just one answer to this question. It really depends on who you ask. Some people will tell you that empaths are born and cannot be nurtured into being or found within oneself. They will tell you it is a gift.

Others will tell you we all have the potential to develop these types of skills and that they can learn to find them in themselves and be taught to use them. Still, others will tell us that it is a combination of both. In a later chapter, we will look at the scientific data supporting the existence of empaths. In this chapter, we will address the question of nature versus nurture; types of empaths; myths about empaths and training for the known empath.

Nature or Nurture?

Let's look first at those who believe that being an empath is a function of nature. You are born with this gift. Most people who hold this conviction also label the empath as "psychic". This causes some concern because there are a lot of ordinary, everyday people that are empathic but don't claim and don't want to claim the psychic label. It's scary because our culture shuns and laughs at most things called psychic.

Being an empath is something you can be born with and maybe we are all born with that ability, but some people have more if it than others right from the beginning. Some people were born with a full-fledged ability to feel the emotions of others "as if they were their own emotions". A lot of born empaths are not really aware of their abilities and gifts until puberty and the onslaught of gender-based hormones.

An empathic child might be shy, quiet or sensitive. They might be confused by what they feel and by how others react to what they feel. What these children or teenagers feel is not the normal empathic reaction the rest of us have. Most of these children will have to learn how to use their gift safely. They need to learn how to block out the rest of the world or they will be feeling everyone's feelings all the time.

Everyone can experience empathy but not everyone is an empath – particularly a psychic empath. The ordinary feeling of empathy allows

16

one to relate to the other person's emotions. The empath feels them in an intense way. The empath must learn to sort out their own emotions from those of others in their vicinity. After this, they can learn to block the other's emotions.

Then there is the school of thought that says this is potential in everyone and the gift has to be nurtured. At the same time, most of the world's cultures don't take anything psychic seriously. However, it is possible that we all have these types of gifts and we simply need to believe it, nurture them and believe in ourselves.

At this time only 5% of the world's population is known to be empathic with an ability to sense the emotions of others on a very high level. They can understand the other on an intimate level because they feel what the other feels. It does not seem like something we can develop, but many believe it is. Many believe that the true empath will suffer from the suffering, will grieve with the grieving and will be ill with those who are ill.

All of these things are simply vibrations of energy and if you can learn to sense that energy, tap into it, then you will be able to pick up on what others are going through. The question will be, do you want to. What is the cost of being a high functioning empath?

Empaths listen well, comfort well, and offer help where they can. This work can cut right through all your defenses. It's very hard for the empath to keep up a high level of this kind of work. You will get tired and lose your energy. Sometimes empaths lose their sense of themselves. This gift is a blessing sure. This gift can be a curse.

Types of Empaths

There are several different types of empaths, though they could all fall into the category of psychic empaths. The difference is the way they receive information from other people's feelings. Some picked them up from objects, some sensed them from people around them. Some help to heal people by working with their subject's feelings and energy.

1. *Emotional* – Feels others' emotions as your own.
2. *Physical/Medical* – Feel others physical pain in your body/healing energy.
3. *Intuitive/Claircognizant* – Knowing without being told.
4. *Animal* – Communication with animals through any of Clair-senses
5. *Clairaudience* – Hearing tones or words.
6. *Telepathic* – Read minds in common parlance or any other the Clair-senses
7. *Plant* – Communication with plants through any of Clair-senses.
8. *Geometric/Environmental/Earth* - – Communication with the earth through any of Clair-senses/energy/signals.
9. *Spiritual*
10. *Clairsentience* – knowing through touch or objects.
11. *Synesthesia* – Multiple senses working together.
12. *Clairvoyance – Seeing lights, images, colors.*
13. *Heyoka* – Indigenous Peoples

Myths about Empaths

1. *Empaths are self-absorbed.*

The truth is that Empaths can be very quiet and often moody. This can look like they are self-absorbed, but in reality, they are absorbed by the emotions of others. The Empath is burdened with feeling other people's emotions as if they were their own emotions.

2. Empaths suffer from mental illness.

The truth is Empaths attract negative energy and can be unbalanced psychologically because of it. This makes them appear depressed or mentally ill to some. Empaths do carry a tremendous amount of baggage emotionally that comes from other people.

3. Empaths are frail and fragile psychologically.

The truth is that Empaths are programmed biologically (nature) for sensitivity and to be in tune with their environment. They carry with them psychologically all the emotions, tensions and energy of other people. They may appear more fragile, may cry more easily when they are really very strong. A lot of Empaths feel so deeply that ordinary activities are impossible for them to participate in. Movies they can't watch because of violence or emotional overload. Contrary to the myth, they are very strong emotionally and mentally.

4. Empaths are lazy.

The truth is that Empaths spend so much energy on the feelings of others, they have no energy left for their own. Empaths are often afflicted with headaches, Chronic Fatigue Syndrome, Fibromyalgia, and insomnia. All the stress that the empath carries will certainly take a toll on their bodies.

5. Only some people have psychic ability.

The truth is that everyone has some psychic abilities even if they are completely dormant. Some people just don't pay attention to the perceptions that are there. Other people are more open and can develop their abilities more easily. Even though all of us have psychic abilities not everyone has the personality to be an empath.

6. *Psychic ability is supernatural, not normal.*

The truth is that psychic abilities are normal, not supernatural. Psychic abilities are the same as any of your other senses. They really are extra senses, yet they are as human as touch, sight, taste. They are physical and as we saw in chapter 3, simply a part of our biological and neurological systems.

7. *If you are psychic your ability unconditional and has no limits.*

The truth is that psychic abilities are like all other human abilities. They are influenced by many things in our human environment. Just as a vision has its limits so too does any psychic sense. If you are in a state of shock or trauma, you might not see what is in front of you or hear what someone is saying to you. The same is true with psychic abilities. You might not be able to pick up other feelings if yours are so traumatized by what is happening to you. The more relaxed you are the more you will pick up and the accurate your "reading" of another will be.

8. *All psychics can see into the future.*

The truth is that though some people do have premonitions, this is not very common among psychic abilities. More often then, not the psychic ability in play is the acquisition of already available information by remote means. I don't need to have a premonition to know you are

20

divorcing your spouse if that information is being broadcast from you to my empathic senses. It is much more common to experience telepathy or clairvoyance than it is to experience premonitions.

Again, we are just touching the surface, the tip of the iceberg in respect to all the myths that are out there about empaths and psychic abilities. Our intention is to simply open you up to all the false information and beliefs that can affect your ability to tap into your empathic nature.

Training an Empath

So, can an empath be trained? Absolutely. We all have dormant abilities to be an empath – to feel the emotions, thoughts and physical sensations of other people. Very often our culture is so loud, moves so fast and is so chaotic, that many will just shut down their sensitivity. It is too much to handle for most people.

Today's empath must struggle with the same stresses of daily life that the rest of us have a plus deal with all the emotions and feelings of the people around them. We are constantly bombarded with external stimuli and Nanosecond technologies. We are attached to our phones, televisions, watches, and laptops.

This situation is much worse for empaths than everyone else. Under these circumstances, the empath tends to distance themselves from themselves. It is very difficult for today's empath to remain functioning, healthy adult. Even empaths can block out some of the noise if you know how It is important for empaths to have boundaries or screens they can put up when all the stimuli become too much.

If an empath has blocked their access to all stimuli and no longer functions as an empath, it can be dangerous to their physical and emotional health. It is important to learn how to live with the dichotomy of feeling other's emotions and staying whole. So the first training must be with empaths who have blocked their sensitivity.

How Empaths Block their Sensitivity

Just like anyone else who wants to block their feelings the empath can do so with actions that suppress feelings. These can include:

Binging – either overeating or under eating. For many, this behavior represents control over one aspect of their lives when all else feels out of control.

Addictive behaviors – eating sugar or caffeine; smoking; alcohol; sex; drugs or adrenaline high.

Emotional eating – swallowing your feelings along with others.

Avoidance of situations, activities or people.

Physical Response to Suppressed Emotions

The empath who suppresses their feelings and blocks their sensitivity to others can suffer from a wide variety of ailments. These could include:

Digestive issues

Chronic Fatigue – with cause

High Blood pressure

Headaches or migraines

Insomnia or sleeping too much

Over the top emotional reactions to ordinary events

Mental and Emotional Response to Suppressed Emotions

Anger and rage

Blaming, critical behavior

Depression/unhappiness

Apathy or lack of emotion

Obsessive-compulsive behaviors

Negative self-talk

Confusion and inability to concentrate

We will talk more about blocking your sensitivity when we look at the experiences of growing up as an open and acknowledging empath in chapter six.

It is important for the empath to let themselves feel the discomfort of their gift in order not to suppress it. Ways to do this include:

- First, teach the empath about the benefits of not hiding their feelings or blocking others. Teach them to identify their emotions separate from others and how to integrate theirs and respond appropriately to the others.
- Provide the empath with examples and models they can follow of others who have allowed their empathy to show through. You can use readings, videos or actual people as these examples. These examples would include positive response to empathy and

also times when the model does not show empathy. Discuss what would happen if the model responded differently.

- Practice empathy and being open to others' feelings without being overwhelmed. Take it a little at a time. Don't give the empath too much to process too quickly or they could completely withdraw.
- Finally, give the empath all the positive feedback you can but also include constructive criticism on how to open up and handle all the emotions better. Information on how to identify and assess other's emotions and respond appropriately.

Empathy can be trained, but it takes a lot of effort on behalf of the trainer and the empath. The example we have given here is of an empath who has blocked their ability and sensitivity in order to protect themselves. This is exactly what happens with 95% of us who are not declared to be empaths. The difference is we do not know we are blocking our empathic abilities due to cultural and social influences and more.

Each of us could benefit from the kind of training outlined above to open our minds and hearts to the empathy we were born with. As previously stated, chapter six, Growing Up Empathic, will cover more on training gifted children to live with and moderate their empathic gifts.

3 CHAPTER 3

The History of Empaths

What is the history of empathy and empaths? Do they have a long history and are there famous empaths that we would all know about? Let's take a look.

History of Empathy and Empaths

What is the history of empathy – an empath? Where does the word even come from and what do we know about empaths throughout history? Prior to the early 1900s, there was no word "empathy" in the English language. The Germans had a word – Einfühlung – whose literal translation is "feeling-in". There were other English translations floating around at the time, until a couple of Cambridge and Cornell psychologists, looked at the Greek translation of "em" and "pathos" empathos = falling-in. Greek for in is em and for feeling is pathos. Thus we have empathos or empathy.

At the time, Einfühlung or empathy meant to project your own feelings onto something or someone else. It did not mean to pick up on the other's feelings. IT was not until the mid-1900's that psychologists began to look at the relationships in society through a scientific lens. Psychologists began working with sociologist and their perspective on empathy began to change.

In the mid-1900s sociologist, Leonard Cottrell was mentoring experimental psychologist Rosalind Dymond Cartwright on ways to measure empathy between people. While doing this work, Cartwright began to change the meaning of "empathy" in order to stress the interpersonal connection. This lets other psychologists separate *projection* from *empathy* – as we know these two concepts today.

This was best defined in a 1955 edition of *Reader's Digest* as – Empathy – "the ability to appreciate another person's feelings without becoming so emotionally involved that your judgment is affected." Today empathy is studied more in neuroscience and primatology than psychology. We will cover this aspect of the history of empaths in Chapter 4 when we look at the science of mirror neurons.

Despite these changes in the meaning of the word empathy from psychologists, there is still a lot of controversy and debate about what empathy really is today. The science has its critics, as does psychology.

26

Arguing against the neuroscientists, psychologists have challenged the location of neurons in the brain, as well as the definition of empathy. Let's leave that discussion for the next chapter. For the sake of history let us use the definition of empathy as the ability to feel what another is feeling from within that other person's frame of reference rather than our own. To walk in another's shoes and literally feel what another feels

In ancient times those who felt this empathy were often referred to as mystics, psychics, seers, priestesses, and priests; before Christianity was even a factor in human life, there were empaths. You can even see this in the Old Testament portion of the bible. It is filled with seers, prophets, and shamans. Long before there was any science to back it up, people experienced themselves or others to be psychic empaths.

Examples of this are the Greek Oracle of Delphi, Samuel in the Old Testament with King Saul and Amos as the seer for Amaziah. At the Egyptian temples, the priest of Ra were seers and in Assyria, the Nabu were seers as well. Psychic empaths, seers, prophets, and shamans have been a part of human history almost since known history began.

Even so, the real flowing of the concept and the experience began in the 1970s and '80s. It was then that the empath was separated out from other types of psychics and psychic behaviors. Going back to nature versus nurture debate, most of us have some amount of this ability to be an empath. It is just more developed in some than in others.

Remember, we are all capable of feeling "empathy" for others. This does not make us an "empath." We can feel empathy without picking up the actual feelings of the other, the non-verbal cues, the knowledge that the other is in pain, or afraid, or happy.

The empath has the ability to just know how the other is really feeling even if the other is attempting to hide their feelings from everyone. Many empaths today will be found in the helping professions. They may be ministers, social workers, counselors or do body/energy work like Reiki.

In the past, the experiences of these people might have gone unnoticed as there was no documenting of them. Because of this, the concept of an empath has been seen as pseudo-science, myth, or just plain made up. For many, the idea itself has had no legitimacy. It is only recently that the role of the true empath has been acknowledged on a broad scale and studied scientifically. Because of this, we are sure there are many empaths in history that we will never be aware of because their stories are lost, or their gifts were not developed. However, there are some historical empaths that we are aware of.

Famous Empaths through History and Those who Influenced Empaths

We will try to make this as chronologically correct as possible. All of the persons mentioned here had a major role to play in the development and acceptance of empaths in history. These people have been open about being empaths or they have embraced the existence of empaths and written or spoken about empathy. Some mentioned here have helped others to manage their own empathic abilities.

Wolfgang Kohler: an American psychologist educated in Germany. He believed that empathy was more of a cognitive gift than a feeling/emotional one. He co-founded the Gestalt School of Psychology.

Edith Stein: A German Nun and philosopher who believed that empathy was the experience of foreign consciousness – in other words, the consciousness of another.

Carl Rogers: An American clinical therapist and psychologist who was a major figure in the exploration of empathy within psychological circles and a lot of the work in the field was his work.

Heinz Kohut: Another American clinical psychologist, he was with the Chicago Institute for Psychoanalysis and was the first and foremost to bring the concept of empathy into the field of psychoanalysis and consider it a scientific activity.

Martin Hoffman: An American professor at NYU (New York University) in the Psychology Department who saw empathy as a biological function leading people to altruism.

Frans de Waal: A Dutch Ethnologist and Primatologist who is in Atlanta as the Director of the Living Links Center within the Yerkes National Primate Research Center. He has written a very influential book entitled "The Age of Empathy".

The following famous empaths are not in any chronological order, but each had a major impact on what empathy and empaths are considered to be in today's culture.

- *Nostradamus* – One of the first really well-known physic empaths. Feeling the pain of the world around him, he engaged in prophecies of its future.

- *Julius Caesar* – though controversial, there is a belief that he was a powerful empath, displayed by his ability to "feel" his way to victory in battle.

- *Edgar Cayce* – one of the world's best-known psychic empaths. Like Nostradamus, he was led to make prophecy based on what he "felt".

- *Caroline Myss* – She became well known as a psychic empath in the 1990s and early 2000s. She did medical intuitive interventions and workshops before fame caught up with her.

- *Henry David Thoreau* – A nature empath he felt the joy and pain of all creation around him. He was known to say, "Could any greater miracle happen than for us to look through each other's eyes for even an instant?"

- *Elizabeth Thomas* – Most people don't know her, but she wrote that "Empathy is the only real human superpower – it can shrink distance, cut through social and power hierarchies, transcend differences, and provoke political and social change.

- *Dr. Michael Smith* – Considered a contemporary empathy guru, he is the author of "The Complete Empath Toolkit". His focus is on those who are aware of their natural empath gifts and want to learn how to use them while protecting themselves from overstraining through shielding.

- *Gandhi* – We are almost all familiar with the story of Gandhi who felt the pain of the Indian people so deeply, he gave his life to change it. He internalized his people's struggle and felt their pain intensely.

- *Martin Luther King* – Whatever you say about Gandhi and the Indian people can be said about MLK and his African American people. He wept for their pain and in the end, gave his life for them.

- *Jane Goodall* -Certainly Jane felt the pain of the chimpanzee and still does. Her empathy for all primates has taught us much about ourselves and our primate brothers.

- *Mother Teresa* – Perhaps the picture of empathy in today's world would be Mother Teresa walking the streets of Calcutta and embracing the unembraceable. She felt the pain of those trapped in India's caste system and those untouchables. This experience led her to feel and respond to the pain of the poor and disenfranchised anywhere in the world that she encountered them.

- *Teresa Caputo* – The Long Island Medium is certainly a psychic/medium empath. She feels deeply the pain of those who ask her help to connect with a loved one who has passed on and to heal some of their pain.

31

We realize this only breaks the surface of famous empaths throughout history. Certainly, you could include Jesus of Nazareth in this listing as well. He felt the pain of all those around him, all the time. He took on the pain of all those around him. Mohammed as well would be called an empath today as deeply as he felt the pain of his people. Buddha? Empathy is certainly a stage or a consequence of enlightenment.

Empathy and empaths are present in all the world's major religions. All three of these historical figures certainly used their gifts in an attempt to make life better for all of us. All three were known to preach love and empathy not just for your friends but for your enemies as well.

In the next chapter, we will look at the science of empaths and empathy and here we will meet more people playing a major and historic role in the development of empaths, empathy, and knowledge around those who actively practice it. This will include scientists, neurologists, psychologist, and psychiatrists, as well as their research and teaching assistants.

Scientists and medical researchers like Kristof and Bloom, or the social Psychologist C. Daniel Baston, who has led the research in this field for many decades are prominent today. Baston especially expands the definition of empathy and empaths saying there are at least eight separate types of concepts referred to as empathy. This includes:

- Knowing the feelings and thoughts of another person.
- Imagining the feelings and thoughts of another person.
- Actually, feeling in your own spirit and body the feelings and thoughts of another person.
- Imagining how you would feel in the other person's situation.

- Actually, feeling pain and distressing yourself because of another's situation.
- Compassion – feeling FOR another's suffering = perhaps more sympathy than empathy.
- Projection – Projecting yourself into the situation of another person.

All this means is that the definitions and the expressions of what empathy is and what it means to be an empath have changed some over time. However, the same need to protect oneself as an empath, the ability to feel what others actually feel is still at the core of what it means to be an empath.

4 CHAPTER 4

The Science of Empathy and Empaths

Is there science behind the concept of empathy and empaths? Is it real science or pseudo-science? Who embraces it and who are the scientists who practice it? All indications say yes there is definitely a science and it has truly come to the forefront of the discussion these days. This is partly because so many people these days consider themselves to be empaths. At the same time, many world leaders in statesmanship, religion, culture, and sciences have come to believe that empathy is critical to a healthy society and to healthy interpersonal relationships.

With empathy, we can share our needs, experiences, and desires and we can build pro-social behavior. With empathy, we can perceive other's emotions and connect with them both cognitively and emotionally. It allows us to "see" the other's perspective and still maintain a division between theirs and others. When emotional empathy is not possible for whatever reason, be it physical, racial, religious, or ethnic, then cognitive empathy must come into play.

Science is now much more positive toward empathy due to the results of newer research in the field of neurobiology. The perception of empathy has changed. It was once thought of as a soft skill but is now considered a neurobiological competency. Neurological research on the brain, through MRIs, has shown that empathic people have a distinct neural relay mechanism that lets the empath unconsciously imitate the facial expressions, mannerisms, and postures of others The same studies show that non-empaths do not show this same neural relay. This is a mirroring response. A good example of this is when the arm of a person in the presence of the empath, is scratched with a needle, the empaths brain registers a response in the same sensory and motor areas as the one who is scratched.

Another study found that when an empath says, "I feel your pain", they really do and it registers in their brain scans. A study was done with a group of volunteer women who received slight shocks to their hands while having brain scans. The scan showed that the area of the pain matrix in their brains was activated when shocked. When told that their spouses had received the same shock, a very similar area of their pain matrix was activated, indicating that the empathy they felt was based in the neurobiology of the women.

The Science of Empathy

There are five aspects of the science of empathy that I want to touch on here without making it all too complicated for most of us. There have been several studies and published results and articles to show that when an empath is feeling another person's feelings there are actual changes in the neurological pathways in the brain. These are the five aspects of the science of empaths that we will explore just a little.

- Mirror Neurons

- Electromagnetic Fields

- Emotional Contagion

- Dopamine Sensitivity

- Synesthesia

Within the brain, it has been discovered that there is a region known as the right supramarginal gyrus. This part of the brain recognizes when we are not using empathy and corrects that for us. If you have to make a decision under pressure or quickly science has found that our capacity for empathy is reduced. The right supramarginal gyrus helps us to know the difference between your feelings and those of other people. Empathy, sympathy, and compassion come from this part of the brain. This part of the brain can differentiate between others and ourselves. In the research, the neurons in this area were intentionally disrupted. When this happened the research participants could not distinguish as easily between their own feelings and those of another person.

Mirror Neurons

Scientific researcher, Max Planck, and his team conducted these experiments, discovering the exact location of the brain where empathy would initiate. They found that to elicit an empathetic response the empath must be stimulated both visually and tactically. If either stimulus was missing the subject could not evaluate the other persons' situation accurately. This study along with the work of Marco Iacoconi, neuroscientist, is making all scientific disciplines, including psychology and sociology, look again at how we understand imitation, empathy, culture, language, autism, and philosophy.

This is due to Iacoconi's discovery of the "smart brain cells" – the mirror neurons. These neurons are what allows human beings to understand other human beings. These mirror neurons seem to be relevant to all areas of humanities shared life and social cognition. From this revolutionary work comes a whole science of empathy and our brain's ability to "mirror" that of another's.

This is not the whole answer as others in the field still debate what this might really mean. Like all other scientific and academic work, this research and the science that arises from it certainly has its critics. Critics wonder if this mirroring property is really empathy, to begin with. Excitement for this field of research is at an all-time high from neuroscientists to psychotherapists, all are attempting to find the secret to human empathy.

These mirror neurons seem to be responsible for empathy and compassion. They "mirror" the thoughts and feelings of the other, be that joy, fear or pain. It is now thought that empaths' mirror neurons were "hyper-responsive". It was also found that it the "other" that triggers these neurons into action. Hearing a puppy whine or a child cry, seeing how happy a friend is, - elicits a deep response in the empath to care for that person or puppy.

On the other hand, think of those who lack empathy – the sociopath, the psychopath, the narcissist – seem to have underactive mirror cells and cannot feel empathy for the other.

Electromagnetic Fields

Another interesting recent discovery is that the heart and the brain of humans produces an electromagnetic field. It is believed that these fields can carry our emotions, thoughts, etc. It is also believed that empaths are highly sensitive to these fields and can be overwhelmed when picking up what is in these fields. Empaths also feel more strongly the changes in the electromagnetic fields of the earth or the sun. These changes can make an empath feel ill or tired. This proves that human being does respond to changes in the climate and seasons.

Emotional Contagion

The next scientific finding that changed the way researchers looked at empaths is called emotional contagion. This does mean what it sounds like – your emotions are contagious and I, an empath, can pick them up. We tend to "catch" one another's feelings. Since this is true of all humans, how much more must it affect the empath? All the more reason to surround yourself with people of positive energy and not toxic ones. We will discuss this later.

Increased Dopamine Sensitivity

It is known that the neurotransmitter dopamine, increases the movement and activity of the neurons and causes pleasure. What was discovered is this pleasure response is much more intense in the introverted empath than it is in the extroverted empath. The introverted empath does not need as much dopamine to experience pleasure or happiness. Scientists are thinking that this could explain many things about the introvert – wanting solitude, meditation, reading, listening to music and not going to that party -are more enjoyable than they are for the extrovert.

Synesthesia

Finally, scientists discovered something they call "mirror-touch synesthesia. This synthesis of two separate parts of the brain – such as the sensors for food and the sensors for music is synthesized. When this happens your brain experiences something very different and strange. When listening to music you feel you can taste the notes. When eating breakfast you feel you can hear the music of your food.

What does this mean for the empath? Well, they experience something called mirror-touch synesthesia. They actually feel both their own body sensations and the other's body sensations at the same time. This can easily become overwhelming for the empath. It is so for the empath to become overwhelmed. Imagine felling your own immense grief and someone else at the same time in your body and your emotions. For more information about this check out the work of Judith Orloff, MD – especially her *Empath's Survival Guide: Life Strategies for Sensitive People*. Dr. Orloff is an associate professor of psychiatry at the University of California Los Angles (UCLA).

Just as the "hard sciences" and medical researchers in neurology and neurobiological sciences are quickly becoming more interested in the study of empaths and empathic energy, so too are the scholars in behavioral sciences such as psychology and sociology. Researchers in this field have defined two types of empathy for the sake of research. These types are cognitive and emotional.

Cognitive Empathy – this is about understanding the feelings of the other. You know you can feel them, but can you understand them? This is also called empathy accuracy by many professionals and academics. According to Hodges and Meyer, this cognitive empathy means that one has a "more complete and accurate knowledge about the contents of another person's mind, including how the person feels." They see cognitive empathy as a skill, not a biological imperative. More and more researchers like Hodges and Meyer are building up the findings in this field.

Emotional Empathy – consists of feeling the exact emotion as the other; includes the empaths own distress in response to the other and the feeling of compassion and need to help the other. Research in this field done by Hodges and Myers states that the empaths own distress level doesn't necessarily exactly mirror the persons. There is a positive connection between what the empath feels and their willingness to help the other.

It is also true in the world of psychology and psychotherapy that having a therapist who is an empath is a real gift for the client. Not necessarily for the therapist. Mental health professionals also agree that having a good level of empathy is highly conducive to functioning well in the culture, having better relationships and more people in your life. Lack of empathy is indicative of antisocial behaviors and personalities.

Psychotherapist Carl Rogers, who we discussed in chapter 3's history of empathy, believed that empathy was an important factor in therapy. If the therapist was an empath, had empathy then they would be able to understand their client from the client's own perspective or frame of mind. It is important for the therapist to be accurate in their understanding of the client and think as one person. Then the therapist can check in with the client to make sure his perspective is indeed accurate. In this way, the therapist would be able to assist the client on a much deeper level without making any judgments.

If this is all true, it would follow that you would want the most empathic people as mental health professionals and therapists. However, there is not yet defined as an accurate way of testing the therapist's capacity for cognitive empathy that is not fraught with error and bias. Researchers are

41

still attempting to deal with this, but it certainly has hampered research in empathic accuracy. However more recent research has shifted its premise to the results more than testing the process. These tests focused on the general public and found a disappointing amount of empathic accuracy. This would support the belief that even if empathy is a "born with" for everyone, it is also in need of nurturing for most everyone.

5 CHAPTER 5

Understanding your Potential

As an empath, you have a lot of unlocked potentials. You probably have not scraped the tip of the iceberg on what an empath can do. So, let's start with a little review. What is an empath and how has history and science viewed them up till now?

One of the best definitions of an empath that we found is a person who knows and feels exactly what someone else is feeling without being given that information. It is a person who vicariously tunes into what is going on with another person emotionally.

In chapter one we said that "If you are an empath you can walk into a room full of people and "sense" that someone is hurting badly, or someone is very happy; someone else is scared and yet another person is hopeful and excited. You will "pick up" all these feelings and the energy that goes with them. It is the energy of the person who feels sad, happy, scared, excited that touches you and you feel what they feel. You feel the energy they are giving out."

Just this little bit of information tells us a lot about an empath, the potential, and the danger, for you live with both. Understanding your potential is vital in facing the challenges of being an empath. We looked at the traits of empaths and the different types. Those of you who are blossoming or potential empaths probably saw yourself in these traits.

Chapters two, three and four looked at the questions of where empathy comes from, who is an empath and in chapter four we moved from myth and anecdotal evidence to scientific studies and neurobiological evidence that being an empath is actually a function of neural pathways in the brain.

Now in chapter five, we begin to focus on you – the empath. What are your experiences and your challenges? How do discover and reach your potential? How do you protect yourself from emotional burnout? Then we will look at some things you can do to develop and practice your empathic skills and putting up and taking down your protective shield.

Learning what an Empath can Do

We know what the traits of an empath are, and we know how many different types of empaths there are. So, as an empath just what is it that you can do? What is it that you have to offer the world because you have developed your empathic abilities?

As an empath, you are receiving information about others – human, plant, animal, earth energy – through your normal senses and through your empathic gifts. Information comes to all of us through taste, feel sound, vision, and odors. If we have developed our empathic abilities, these normal sensory perceptions will be quite intense. We all have psychic abilities whether we know it or not, whether we develop them or not. These abilities are manifested first through our normal physical senses.

Since everyone and everything on our planet is interconnected, we all have the ability to reach out and connect with the other. We receive information from this interconnected web every minute of every day, but we might not be aware of it.

The active or developed empath is a little different from this. This person is aware of their empathic ability whether developed or not. They are at least to a small extent "awake". This person can respond to any situation through the 5 physical senses or through their empathic ability. Some choose to use these abilities and others feel that they have no choice. The empathic senses are thrust upon them – which only means that their normal senses respond in an overwhelmingly intense manner.

They walk past an upset person and "hear" what that person is saying to themselves or they "see" what that person is upset about. The information can come through their 5 senses, but it is extrasensory in its intensity and its "knowing without knowing" manner. This is because the empath is so attuned, so sensitive to the mental and emotional aspects of another being. Everyone has this psychic or empathic potential, but not everyone knows how to access it, while others don't know how to turn it off.

So, what do empaths do?

- They "specialize" in communication with people, animals and/or plants.

- Empaths "listen" to that still, small voice within themselves. They listen to that voice in your head – not the one that never stops talking or chattering about life – but the spiritual one – the authentic one. The one many people call God. Others simply call it that still small voice. The one of which we say, "Be still and know".

- This voice is could also be labeled as a conversation with yourself. Your physical self and your spiritual self. Your conscious self and your unconscious self. What empaths do when they listen to this voice may seem like recognizance. It may seem that the voice is telling you what to avoid, what might happen around the next corner.

- Empaths can interpret what this voice is saying and knows what to do with the information. Most of us when hearing this voice can acknowledge it but we just don't know what to do with it. The potential we all hold is in this area. Develop our empathic abilities and we will be able to understand what the still small voice is telling us and what we should do.

So, what is the potential of the empath? What could they do in addition to what they already do? The potential is much more than the emotional interconnectedness of the empath and the other. The empath is capable of a lot more as they grow and broaden their perception and allow in more and more of the other's perceptions.

The potential of the empath as she grows is that in any given situation as she is drawn to one in need, she will be able to approach that person, connect with them and listen to their concerns. She will also find the right message and the right words to comfort the other. This is the first level potential of the empath.

If the empath continues to allow herself to grow and develop her skills while still looking out for herself, her potential to do good in the world is endless. Her potential to communicate with others in need, be they people, animals or the earth itself will continue to develop. She can become a beacon of hope, one person, one being at a time.

While helping others in this way, the empath will increase their own view of the world, their own perspective at the same time. They will become more and more open in the sharing of their empathic gifts. The potential is endless as the empathic gift flows through every part of their life, opening them up more and more as they offer themselves up to more and more.

Practicing Empathic Behavior

So, the key is to develop your empathic gifts, perspectives, and behavior. To do this you need to practice. You need to know how to develop your gifts and how practicing can be a large part of that development plan. In this section, we are going to look at how you can help yourself to become a better empath.

Since we have a whole chapter, chapter eight, devoted to the safety of empaths, we will not deal with that training or practicing here. This section is devoted to the personal growth of an empath. Something you already know a lot about whether you are aware of it or not. As an empath, you already think differently from many around you. You are already the master of your own being as you are willing to be an empath in the face of cultural disbelief and skepticism.

No matter your level of understanding, of training, or of development, you are both already the master of your empathic abilities and in development of them. Let's assume you have an inkling of your empathic self but are not really awakened to it. Here's what you will want to do.

- Open yourself up to your empathic abilities by admitting they exist. Recognize yourself for the empath that you already are. Admit that within your unconscious there is a powerful empath waiting to be nurtured.
  Every once in a while, you hear her, you feel her, you even see her – the empath within you. Acknowledge her and bring her into your consciousness. Keep imagining this empath within you as a gift, a grace and bring her out of the unconscious into consciousness where both you and others can appreciate her. Whatever image you need to use to do this is ok. Imagine bringing your unconscious out of a burning house and into the oxygen-rich air where she can breathe and try.
- Because our unconscious mind is, for the most part, unattainable when we are awake and active when we are asleep, the empath can learn a lot from his dreams. Unfortunately for most of us, when we wake up, we lose the specifics of those dreams. However, it is possible to maintain the essence of dreams and

48

learn from them. Even if we do so on the unconscious level. Try to remember as much as you can. Write it down as soon as you wake up – and especially if you wake up in the middle of the night.

- Your empathic knowledge is always with you in your unconscious mind, but you can bring it to your conscious mind if you choose to and if you practice doing so. Sometimes and for some highly sensitive empaths, that knowledge will present itself without any conscious effort on your part. To increase the chances for this, you need to practice bringing it to your conscious mind. How do you do that?

Here's an easy exercise you can do daily whenever you are around several people. You can do this in your office or the grocery store, in a park or waiting for the movie to start in a theater. Just be calm and take a good look around you. Send out your antenna and try to get a "feel" for the people in this particular group. Don't linger on any one person but try to observe the face of every person in your line of vision. Pay attention to what you feel as you look at each individual. Does anyone, in particular, bother you? Does anyone hurt? Do you feel safe as you do this? Try to "hear" something from the people in the room without interacting with them in any way but looking.

Little by little you will experience more and more empathic emotions as you practice this skill. But be careful. Don't let any toxic or dangerous energy enter your empathic space. If you feel this move away quickly and do not interact with that person. In a later chapter, we will discuss how to protect yourself in that situation. What we are doing now is learning to bring unconscious empathic responses out into the light of consciousness and learn to deal with them.

Once you become "conscious" of the energy in the room, you will be able to "feel" that person walking up behind you before you see or hear them. Your empathic senses will tell you they are there. The more you practice these types of skills the more the world of empathy and "psychic" reality will open up for you. As we saw in chapter four, these "physic" abilities are not "woo woo" type superstitious or even mystical abilities. They are based in neuroscience and are actual, factual functions of the brain. Like any other function of the brain, "practice makes perfect".

Another set of exercise will seem mystical, spiritual or otherworldly to you as it is tied to those rituals people use in prayer and meditation to reach higher states of being. You can increase your empathic knowledge and energy through some of the very same rituals. Things like:

- Mindfulness
- Guided Meditations
- Laying of hands when empathically healing someone as in Reiki
- Talking out loud sends empathic messages as well. Try to listen to others. Listen to your own.
- Practice paying attention to what you "feel" in your body. What is your "gut" saying to you? How does this empathic energy feel in your body? Chills? Tension? Body temperature? How often have you "felt" something but were unable to name it? So often I have said to myself, "Something is bothering me, and I don't know what it is." That is the time to pay attention to their

feelings. Perhaps using mindfulness meditation to just be with the feelings until they tell you what they are all about.

Practice your empathic abilities. Tune into your empathic energy. Listen to your own still quiet voice. In these ways, you will grow, prosper and develop your potential as an empath.

6 CHAPTER 6

Growing up Empathic

Were you born aware of your empathic gift? Did you discover as a young child that things were just a little different for you than for your friends and others around you? Even though every living thing has the potential for physic empathy, some of us were more in tune from birth than most of us.

Growing up in our culture allows children to suppress or forces children to suppress a lot of their empathic unconscious knowledge until much later in life. So many children are born "knowing" and then they suppress their knowledge. We will discuss this in some detail, how they suppress what they "know" and how to help them open up to these gifts again.

Born as an Empath

It is certainly not easy to be "born as an empath" or in other words to be born aware of empathic and psychic energy. You feel something, yet you feel out of place because you know that others around you don't feel the same thing. You have an awareness and a perception of things that others do not have. It may make you appear to be smarter or more intelligent, but that is not what is really going on. Your "knowing" is an empathic, not an intellectual knowing.

I am an animal empath. As an adult, I learned to allow my gifts to open up and to become what our culture is beginning to call an animal communicator. More about this in a later chapter, but the point here is that as a very small child, from age two on, I was in telepathic communication with animals. I knew they were talking to me and I knew they heard what I was saying back to them. I knew where they were when I was not around, and I knew if they would meet me at the door when I got home. Yet I too suppressed this gift until much later in life.

Learning Empathy as a Child

It is when we are children that we first consciously learn about and develop empathy. If we are lucky enough to be surrounded by people who are not afraid to show empathy, whether they understand it as a psychic gift or not, we can learn it from them. If we experience empathy from others, we will learn how to show it ourselves and how to tap into our empathic selves.

This is more difficult in western cultures than it needs to be, but in western cultures emotions are suppressed not valued. Parents do not discuss their own emotions with their children, so children do not become comfortable with emotions. Since emotion is at the heart of empathy, it is difficult for an empathic child to function well, or for another child to learn empathy while suppressing emotion.

One of the best times for teaching children empathy and how to channel their empathic energy is in the face of grief. If a grandparent or a favorite animal companion dies, don't sweep it under the rug. Let your children see your emotions and your responses to the grief of others around you. This is the perfect opportunity to teach children to acknowledge their own emotions and grief, and also to learn how to comfort others in their pain and grief. Yes, your children will feel your pain, the pain of the rest of the family and friends. This is normal grief and will teach your child how to channel and control their own empathic abilities. Talk with your children about how you "feel", how someone else may feel, even how the deceased may feel now that they have passed into the realm of spirit.

Helping a Child Who is Growing Up as an Empath

It's great if a child empath can grow up in an empathic, sensitive or psychic family, but that is not the case for so many. Imagine being raised in an environment where emotional gifts and psychic energy is respected, revered even. Think how much a child would learn to respect and love themselves in that type of environment, instead of learning to doubt, to question, perhaps to hate oneself in a suppressive environment.

Our culture as a whole has little respect for sensitive people, no fewer empaths. In our culture, it is logic and science that rules. Thankfully science is beginning to change the rules around empathy and psychic abilities, understanding that they are hard-wired in all of us. Unfortunately, this message has not reached the general culture where there is a major mistrust of science anyway these days.

So how can you help a child who is growing up in our culture today as an empath? As we wait for our culture to catch up with our science and the cosmic shift that is happening today, how do we protect and assist our empathic children? Do we tell them the stories of old – of shamans, seers, healers -? That would help, but it would not be enough.

Again we are fortunate that this cosmic shift in understanding is bringing us some tools for assisting our children. Judith Orloff, a psychiatrist, is a beacon of hope in this field. She has a test to see if your child or even you, is an empath. She has lots of advice about what to do if they are. She is leading the way, but there are others.

Help your empathic child see her psychic energy as a gift, not a burden or a strangeness. Tell them we ALL have the potential to develop our own empathic/psychic gifts. Help them to see how empathic energy is being brought into the mainstream instead of the shadows. Instead of labeling our children as ADHAD let's name them what they are – empaths.

Help your empathic child to recognize that you support their gifts. Empathy is not as easy as we know. It takes a toll no matter how prepared or self-assured we are. Let's make it just a little easier for our empathic children to adjust. Don't label your children as "emotional", "difficult" or "overly sensitive" when they are in fact young empaths. Children labeled in this way can be damaged for life and might suppress their gifts for life. Help them to appreciate their empathic gift rather than run from it or resent it.

How do you know if your child is an empath or leans toward being one? Look for these signs and then act to help your child.

- Is your child extremely sensitive to the feeling of the others around her? Do they pick up your every concern or worry? Do they know your grief and anger even as you try to keep it from them? You can't lie to an empath. If your child knows your truth that you try to hide from him, you can assume he is an empath.

- Does your child have physical symptoms in response to feelings they can't understand or express? Headaches and stomachache in particular fit in this category. Sympathize and offer kindness. Don't push them to talk about their feelings but if they are open to doing so, listen.

- Does your child have a gut level negative reaction or act out in the presence of certain people? If so, it is likely that they are picking up that person's energy. The energy you cannot feel, and which is frightening or repulsive to your child. Do not force your child to stay in that person's presence just because you are embarrassed. Respect your child's feelings.

- Does your child have unexplained tantrums or excessive shyness? Is moodiness not appropriate to age? Does he shut down? Have trouble focusing? All of these could be signs of an empath in need of help, support, understanding.

- Is your child overly responsible? Are they always trying to help, to fix, to care for others? You might like this in your child and even feel proud of him, but it also may be too much for him to carry. Let them know they are not responsible for grownups problems. Help them to create boundaries and then respect them. Help your child to be a child, to play, have fun, be loved.

Teach your empathic child to cope and thrive before she begins to suppress her empathic self.

7 CHAPTER 7

Using Spiritual Healing Tools

Empaths need spiritual heal tools for two reasons. The first is to care for the other when the empath perceives them to be in intense emotional pain. The second is to care for themselves when they have been exposed to too much intense emotional pain. This is an area where a lot of work has been done and it is not necessary to reinvent the wheel. There are plenty of tools to choose from and enough to meet any need. In this chapter, we will look at the tools, who they can help and how to cultivate them.

First, a few principles to agree on. By now we pretty much know and accept what empathy is. We know there is a basis in scientific fact for empaths. We know that everyone has the potential to be an empath but not everyone will develop this gift. For this reason, many have come to believe that empathy is an inherited trait. It is not unless you are speaking only in an evolutionary model, we are all hard-wired for empathy.

It's in our DNA. We do however need to know what type of empathic energy we have – is it cognitive or empathic. We covered about ten different types of empaths in an earlier chapter. Here is just a quick reminder:

Emotional

Healing

Psychometry

Geomancy

Animal Communication

Telepathy

Mediums

Nature

Precognition – some believe this is an entirely different gift than empathy – some put it here.

Knowing or Claircognizance

No matter the type of empath, most make great doctors, nurses, and physicians assistants. Healing is always a part of the role of an empath. There are different ways to get there, but everyone ends up there in one form or another because healing is what empaths do. So what tools do you bring to this endeavor?

What are the Tools?

Tools for Healing the Other

- Meditation – helping to bring the other to a more peaceful place. Here the empath can help another to find peace, be grounded and protected. Imagine the person who needs healing inside their own bubble, a bubble you created, and you put them there for their protection and healing. You placed them safely into the bubble and brightness of healing energy. No other energy can get in.

- Intentions – if you meditate or do mindfulness work you are familiar with intentions. When you feel the negative energy coming out you, use your intentions to reverse it and send it back out into the universe as healing energy. Use your intentions and your meditation skills to send the healing energy back to the person who is sending out negative energy.

- Laying of hands – we mentioned this at an earlier time, but as an empath when you are connecting with your healing energy and want to assist another, Your healing empathic energy will be more effective with the use of ritual such as healing hands – like with Reiki. First center yourself and then place your hands over the area of the body that needs to heal. Breathe deeply and focus on the energy flowing from the earth into your body; from your hands into the others' body. Feel the energy flow through you.

You can use any imagery you are comfortable with, any prayers or helpers you are comfortable with or you can go it alone. As with Reiki, pass your hands over the person's body a few times, silently calling for her to be calm and relaxed. You may or may not feel where the person needs the most energy, but you should feel your energy release once the healing is done.

If you experience any clear fear-inducing energy while doing this, don't stop immediately, Try putting the bubble around yourself. If this doesn't work and there is too much negative energy, you will have to stop. Remember you must protect yourself in order to assist anyone else.

Tools for Healing Yourself

- Hypersensitivity: When too much is coming at the empath at once, you can become hypersensitive to another's energy. Your body reacts to this stress automatically, intuitively with the fight or flight response. Overcome this hypersensitivity by doing the following:

  Breath is deep as if beginning meditation, center yourself and ask for the balance. If at all possible, take yourself out of the presence of the negative energy and fight off your own hypersensitivity attempting to integrate all you are sensing.

- Use oils, diffusers, incense. crystals, sage – any sacred item that will help you to calm and protect yourself.

- Water is one of the empath's strongest allies. You can use it to calm yourself or for blessing and calming others. Water will create balance. Water should be always with you if you are using healing energy. Just carry a very small bottle of sacred water with you at all times. Apply the water to the third eye of the other or yourself. Apply an intention, such as peace, to the water. How far you need to go depends on how far the hypersensitivity goes. If you just feel some negativity from the person in the room with you, you can deal with it right there. However, if you are so hypersensitive that you can hear the bug walking across the floor -that is hypersensitivity!! Place yourself in the bubble, leave the room and attempt to become ever increasingly calm and quiet.

Other Tools for Taking Care of Yourself

We have touched on some of these tools briefly in other places. Now we will look just a little closer at the spiritual healing tools that are available to you.

1. Smudging or cleansing negative energy – this is a very traditional healing tool for cleansing a person or space. There are a variety of herbs or resins that can be used for this. In western culture, sage is a very popular herb for cleansing. This cleansing makes the space of the person a safe place to be.

2. Affirmations

3. Salt – salt will absorb negative energy. Put a small bowl of sea salts in every room in your house. Carry them with you. They will cleanse the area and you.

4. Bowls, Rattles – noisemakers will vibrate at certain levels and resonate with us at certain levels. Each being, each thing in the universe has its own level of vibration. In order to cleanse your own vibration, you need vibrations that resonate at a level higher than your own. Try different tools and even tuning forks until you find one that resonates for you. Tap the object and let the vibration resonate around you. You will find yourself relaxing into the right vibration.

5. Crystals – these can help to balance your energies, help with healing and help you to balance others' energies.
   - Black Tourmaline – Absorbs negative energy.
   - Rose Quartz – emotional healing, compassion, romance.
   - Apache Gold – boundaries and absorbs negative energy.
   - Ouro Verde Quartz – Protects from excess emotions and energy.
   - Amethyst – healing, emotional protection, spirituality, peace, and calm.
   - Hematite – shields and strengthens auras while avoiding those who drain you.
   - Citrine – purify, heal, happiness, abundance.
   - Aqua Aura Quartz – deflecting and trapping negative energies.

- Quartz – balance, protection, healing, energy.
- Chrysanthemum Stone – Builds a wall to protect your boundaries.
- Flame Aura (Titanium Aura or Titanium Quartz) – Rainbow is a buffer shield to keep out hurtful energies.

6. Essential Oils – these can be used in many ways and for many purposes. Some are used for a blessing when a being is sick. Other ones come in if that being is near passing into spirit. These are healing oils of proven, tremendous power. Which oils do you use for what types of situations? Here are just a few examples.
   - Energy enrichment/increasing – Peppermint, Orange, Eucalyptus, Rosemary, Lemon, Cinnamon, and Ginger.
   - Anxiety Reduction includes – Neroli, Lavender, Rose, Basil, Cedarwood, Chamomile, and Bergamot.
   - Negative Energy Repellents – Citronella, Rosemary, Geranium, Frankincense, Sage, Eucalyptus, Tee Tree, Peppermint and Lavender.

7. Unclutter your life and your space. This might not seem at first glance to be a spiritual healing tool, but it is. Whatever does not serve you in your life should be cleaned out of your life. If you weed your garden healthier plants will grow in more abundance. Unclutter your heart, your mind, your closets, your storage areas and only keep those things physical and metaphysical that serves your life. A good place to start might be with practicing mindfulness and mindfulness meditation.

8. Statements of Intention or Affirmations. Louise Haye taught us about these many, many years ago in respect to our physical

health. They are just as important and powerful in respect to your empathic and spiritual health. They reinforce your beliefs, feed the positive energy, focus the energy and make sure your energy is only being influenced by yourself and no one else.

9. Books, CDs, Music. These are very important tools for spiritual healing and when you are decluttering your life and space, remember that you need these in one form or another. You don't have to have rooms full of bookcases full of old and new spiritual, empathic and scientific books. You can have a kindle full of enticing and enlightening books. You choose them for yourself. I will mention just a few here for you to consider. There are some amazing teachers out there writing amazing books.

- Empath by Alex C. Wolf
- Survival Guide for Empaths Become a Healer Instead of Absorbing Negative Energies by J.P. Edwin
- PSYCHIC PROTECTION CRYSTALS The Modern Guide To Psychic Self-Defense With Crystals For Empaths & Highly Sensitive People by Ethan Lezzerini
- Trust Your Vibes and Diary of a Psychic by Sonia Choquette
- The Beginners Survival Guidebook for Healing a Highly Sensitive Person by Suzanne Cron Heuertz and Ian Christian Stabile
- The Universe Has Your Back: Transform Fear to Faith by Gabrielle Bernstein
- Emotional Freedom: Liberate Yourself from Negative Emotions and Transform Your Life by Judith Orloff -

we have already mentioned Judith in previous sections having to do with the science and history of empaths

- The Complete Empath Toolkit: 44 Steps to Master Your Energy by Michael R. Smith
- Finely Tuned: How To Thrive As A Highly Sensitive Person or Empath by Barrie Davenport
- Dancers Between Realms: Empath Energy - Beyond Empathy by Elisabeth Y. Fitzhugh
- Becoming An Empath by Karla McLaren
- The Highly Intuitive Child: A Guide to Understanding and Parenting Unusually Sensitive and Empathic Children
- by Catherine Crawford

10. Courses – online There are many online courses for empaths and for raising an empathic child. Some of these courses are taught by some of the authors in our book list above. Sonia Choquette and Gabrielle Berstein come to mind immediately but there are so many more. If you like online work rather than or in addition to reading a book, check out all the resources available there. Here are just a few ideas.

- Sonia Choquette | Spiritual Teacher, Author & Consultant

- Judith Orloff MD | Empath Support, Intuition, Emotions

- Gabby Bernstein

- The Empath Academy

- Online Classes for Empaths – Chakra Center

- The Empath's Survival Guide Online Course - Judith Orloff MD

- Empath School | Spirit Heal Institute for Intuition & Healing

  The Enlightened Empath Training

- Empowered Empath Course - Dana Childs Intuitive

- The Empath's Empowerment Online Course | Beacons of Change

It's not easy being an empath. It has its wonderful moments and its devasting times. The energy in the world today is darker than at other times and lighter than at still other times. No matter what it is, the empath will feel it and take into himself. She will either thrive from the energy she receives or drowns in the despair she picks up. Every minute of every day this outside energy is coming at the empath with no end in sight.

You must know how to use spiritual and healing gifts in order to survive; in order to offer any kind of assistance to those whose struggles you feel like your own. That is the point of this chapter and the next one. Learn to feed yourself. Learn to protect yourself. Know what tools are available, what they do, and how to use them. Then use them.

Control the energies coming at you. Build your bubble and stay inside it as long as you need to. Retreat to your safe place whether in your mind or in a physical form. Enjoy the blessings of being an empath who can make a positive difference in this world. Enjoy the blessings of being an empath who can help even one other person or one other empathic child. Enjoy it all but protect yourself from the exhaustion, the stress and the toll being an empath can take on your life.

8 CHAPTER 8

Keeping Yourself Safe – Avoiding Toxic People

Now that we have looked at the spiritual and emotional tools that an empath has to assist him with healing others and being open to using your gifts for those who need you, let's look at how to take care of yourself. It is vital for an empath to be healthy, balanced, and in harmony with all of life in order to be safe and not overwhelmed by other's feelings and needs. Most importantly it is vital for the empath to keep themselves safe and avoid toxic people.

What are or who are toxic people? What makes a person toxic and how can the empath avoid being in contact with them? The worst damage to a sensitive or empath will come from a toxic friendship, so it is important not to enter into the relationship, to begin with. If the people in your life cause you more pain than they give you joy, let them go from your life and your heart. As an empath, you simply cannot afford to be in toxic relationships of any kind.

These relationships are so dangerous because the empath can feel intensely all the negativity, hate and venom in the heart of a toxic person. Being in their presence is intensely painful and devastating for the empath. A really sensitive empath might be rendered incapacitated by being in the presence of a toxic person.

Recognizing Toxicity in People

How can the empath recognize toxic people before becoming influenced by them? What should an empath be looking for or open to in order to identify and move away from toxic people?

- Anyone who makes you feel bad about yourself is toxic.
- Sarcasm is a weapon. Don't let it be used against you.
- The toxic person is manipulative. They try to make you feel bad about you – to doubt your feelings, your intuition.
- The toxic person creates chaos and makes reality seem crazy. They make you feel their craziness. It then becomes the empaths own. You take on their craziness and they know exactly what they are doing.
- Toxic people respect no boundaries. They occupy your personal space and disrespect any boundaries you attempt to build.

- Trust your gut – your intuition – when you feel you are not safe then you are not safe. Watch for the red flags. They will be there.
- Most toxic people enjoy getting under your skin and into your empathic heart. They enjoy messing you up. They are very cruel and very dangerous. They have to diminish you in order to feel better about themselves. Pay attention and move away from this type of behavior.
- Toxic people play with the emotions of others. The better they know you the more they will play with hurting you and it is intentional and enjoyable for them.

How an Empath Experiences Toxic People

- Shutting down – if the empath is too scared, too traumatized by the toxic person, they tend to shut down, to withdraw, to hide their real selves, their personalities.
- Exhaustion – many empaths feel exhausted in the presence of toxic people. If the toxic person is just going on and on, they are zapping your empathic energy and your physical energy.
- Being with a toxic person can cause an empath to become bitter or angry and not even be in touch with why they feel that way. The real evil and danger here are that these feelings can stay with the empath long after they are no longer in the presence of the toxic personality.
- Physical symptoms such as headaches, nausea, inability to concentrate and just feeling "wrong" or just "not feeling right".
- Feeling apathetic – not caring about anything.

- Getting seriously ill.

If you experience any of these things- run as fast as you can in any direction other than where the toxic personality is. Start building your protections. Start defining your sacred space and moving into it. Create a safe space for yourself. Inviolate space for yourself – a place to retreat to. There are things you can do to protect yourself, but it begins with a safe place – somewhere to get completely away from any toxic people in your life.

You have to find or create your own sacred space. Sacred space is somewhere to center yourself, ground yourself, recompose yourself. So how does one go about finding or creating this sacred space?

Sacred Space

It doesn't have to be a place it can be in your mind. It can be anything you want or need it to be. It just has to work. If you can create a sacred space in your mind and go there entirely when you are still physically in the presence of the toxic person, do it. Most empaths cannot do this. Most will need a real physical sacred space that you can go to and get center, renewed and recreated.

Just remember the goal is to reconnect with yourself, your heart, your empathic soul. To do this you have to put yourself at the center of that sacred space and build out from yourself whatever you need in that space. It could be that you don't need anything at all in that space. Just a place to reconnect, to refill your tank with intuition, imagination, energy, and love. If you have a sacred space to come home to, you will be able to get rejuvenated to go back out and help those who need your empathic support.

Some things you can do in sacred space:

- Make an altar in your sacred space for prayer, meditation, reflection.
- Add a cushion, a blanket, music, a journal. Maybe you want a candle, a diffuser, smudge.

Now add the other possible tools that might keep you safe –

- A shield or cloak to put between ourselves and the other.
- Walks in the woods or along the beach to re-center yourself.
- Taking breaks from being with too many people and certainly from being with toxic people.
- Headphones for either listening to music or guided meditations.
- Foods that ground you might include nuts, root vegetables, juice, bread.
- Be intentional. Start every day with an intention for that day.

A few more tools:

Be able to express what you feel and what you need. Know what you need. Know what you feel. Be able to express what you need and what you feel.

Visualize your shield – You need a shield that will allow your positive energy to flow while blocking any toxic energy out. Design your shield so that you can put up the wall quickly while seeing the wall being able to breathe with the positive energy.

Set boundaries whether the toxic person will respect them or not. You can defend and demand them. You can put in earbuds if you are in the presence of the toxic person and they will not give up talking at you. Whatever you need to do to set limits and stick to them.

Drink a lot of water. Be good to yourself. Meditate, meditate, meditate…yes, meditate. Meditation will calm you down. The mediation will lower your heart rate, slow down your breathing. Meditation will let you step into your emotional sacred space, your safe place. Meditation is the empaths best friend.

A lot of the tools and skills we mentioned in the previous chapter are also vital resources here for empaths dealing with toxic people. You need spiritual healing tools and a place to retreat to. You need to be able to place the bubble over yourself and not let anyone or any energy in. Many of the resources in terms of crystals, essential oils, meditations, affirmations, smudging, and sacred water. Find yourself some holy ground and hold it. Don't stand down. Don't give it away.

Toxic people could literally kill you. Don't let them. Be strong. Use your smarts and your reputation to keep yourself alive. Here are just a few tools of your own for dealing with the toxic personality.

1. Books
    - Toxic People: 10 Ways of Dealing With People Who Make Your Life Miserable
      by Lillian Glass

74

- Setting Boundaries: Learn When To Say Yes And No (Difficult People, Empath, Saying No, Survival Manual, Toxic People) by Kristine S. Everest
- Empath Protection by David C. Walter
- Awakened Empath: The Ultimate Guide to Emotional, Psychological and Spiritual Healing by Aletheia Luna and Mateo Sol
- Self-Care for the Self-Aware: A Guide for Highly Sensitive People, Empaths, Intuitive, and Healers by Dave Markowitz
- Empath: 2 Books in 1: A Comprehensive Guide For Highly Sensitive People And How Empaths Can Protect From Narcissistic Abuse by Judith Goleman
-

2. Online Courses
    - Protecting Yourself - Michael Smith
    - Essential Energy Care for Empaths - Mark Youngblood
    - Empath Training: Learn How to Control and Develop Your Gift
    - Empowered Empath - Lone Wolf

9 CHAPTER 9

Unusual Empaths

We touched on a lot of different traits and abilities of empaths, and we have also listed and briefly discussed the different types of empaths. In this chapter, we will look more closely at some of the more unusual empaths. When most people think of empaths or psychics, they think of human to human empathic energy and abilities. However, there are those empaths with special callings or special relationships with the non-human world. There may or may not be as many of them as there are human-human, but they are a fascinating group to explore.

We will be looking at three such types in this chapter – the animal empath, the plant empath, and the earth empath.

Animal Empath/Fauna

There are those who have a special connection with animals, and we call those animal empaths, but some go even farther. Some have special connections with ALL living things – animals, insects, plants, etc. We will mostly look at the Animal Empath here, but keep in mind, many if not most animal empaths have a connection with insects as well.

What does it mean to be an animal empath? Pretty much the same thing it means to be any type of empath. The animal empath faces a few more challenges when confronted with skeptics and non-believers. This is because to be an animal empath you have to know that animals have emotions, intelligence, and capabilities beyond what human scientists, psychologists, philosophers, and theologians have assigned to them. If animals are not capable of true emotions beyond instinct, then there can be no such thing as an animal empath.

However, we know better. Even today many of the scientists, psychiatrists, philosophers, and theologians know better. Even the Old Testament says that animals have souls. Can they have souls but not be able to experience real love? It seems preposterous to those of us who are empaths and probably to anyone who lives with an animal. It is well known today that elephants have emotions, intelligence and probably are empaths themselves. The same can be said of dolphins, whales, many primates, and even canines – including your dog.

So, given this as fact instead of fiction, an animal empath has the ability to feel, understand, and communicate the feelings, thought processes and state of mind of animals. In our chapter on the history of empaths and historical figures who were empaths, we did not touch on the animal empath very much.

Certainly, there have always been animal empaths even though the way we live with animals today is drastically different than humans did at other times. In certain times the only people who were close to nature were witches, heretics or lunatics. If what you thought about animals or nature was not in lockstep with the doctrine of The Church, you could be burned at the stake for your beliefs. Yet in the midst of these times, we find the most famous of all animal empaths and a Catholic monk at that. Anyone who loves animals is familiar with the history and the stories of St. Francis of Assisi. He could "talk" with the animals and his reputation was impeccable.

Perhaps because he founded three religious orders – the Order of Friars Minor (the Franciscans), the Order of St. Clare and the Third Order of St. Francis – had a reputation for goodness and purity, his gift as an animal empath was met with honor, not an accusation. He was considered holy not a witch and his gift came from God, not some demonic presence.

The most famous story of St. Francis is his taming of the wolf that was terrorizing the village of Gubbio. This relationship with the wolf was considered to be a miracle. Yet he also "talked" with birds and squirrels and all manner of wild creatures. They were said to sit on him and eat out of his hands as he preached the Gospel to them.

It is true that he spent more time with animals than with men as he was a very solitary, spiritual person. Did this allow him to develop this empathy with the animals or was he born with it? Do we all have the ability if we open ourselves up to it? Many of us are animal empaths. If St. Francis lived today, he would be considered an "animal communicator" as well as an animal empath. An animal communicator has the abilities of an animal empath and they may be the same. Or the difference may be that the animal communicator has opened themselves up to the telepathic language that all animals speak.

It is not hard to communicate with animals telepathically if we are open to it. Yet it is so unusual for humans that most animals are very surprised to hear us talk to them that way or to know that we can actually hear them. Many, many animals simply consider human beings to be deaf when it comes to hearing them in their own voices. The more the person interacts with animals on this non-verbal level, the better they get at it and the strong their empathic interactions with animals become.

Within the community of animal communicators, there are those whose abilities are tied to their physical senses in the same way any empath is. Some "hear" the animal's messages in their minds, Some "see" visions or pictures sent from the animals. Others still feel in their bodies what the animal is feeling and saying. Some can diagnose an animal's illness. Some need to actually touch an animal to communicate while many just reach out across distances with their hearts and minds. In the end, it is not at all different than what all the other empaths do.

Animal empaths are blessed with being able to really feel all the unconditional love that animals have to offer. They do this at a much deeper level than most of us do with the animals we live with. And they understand them at a much deeper level with a very deep mutual respect between the animal and the empath. This is a blessing indeed. When you consider all the stress and the overwhelmingness of being an empath, then being able to absorb all this love coming from their animal companions is a much-appreciated gift.

The animal empath is nurtured by being with them, while any empath can be completely drained by being with people. Which explains a saying I saw once – Animals Forever. People, Whenever. This just might sum up how many animal empaths feel. So if you are an animal empath what can you do with this gift? Well as mentioned just above, you can become an animal communicator. Read one or more of the many books written by animal communicators or take an online course. Longtime animal communicator Penelope Smith keeps a directory of worldwide professional animal communicators and she has written many books on the subject.

You could simply volunteer to work with animals. There are many ways to do this. Many shelters need volunteers, many zoos and aquariums too. You can train service animals, foster rescues, or become a handler for a search and rescue dog. Or take it one step further and become a trainer yourself. There are many ways to use your gifts.

Plant Empath/Flora

So, an exceptionally close relationship with animals is not your calling as an empath. You feel much closer to anything that grows – plants, flowers, trees. This makes you a Plant Empath or a Flora Empath and there are probably less of these even than animal empaths. Now you may say what are you talking about? Didn't you just say that to be an animal empath you have to acknowledge that animals have feelings and intelligence beyond what humans have credited them with? Are you telling me plants have feelings and trees are intelligent?

Well, yes kind of. Plants need and thrive on certain things and the plant empath is somehow in touch with these needs and wants. The plant empath has a "green thumb" because somehow, they "know" that this plant like to sit in that window and none other even though the sunlight is the same in other windows.

We now know that plants respond to music and human voices. Why would they not respond to a person who understood them inherently? But do the plants and trees talk back? Do they share their feelings? Scientists are now saying that trees and plants may indeed have feelings. Many plant empaths have shared stories of feeling the intense pain or need of a tree that was being strangled by vines or wire.

Knowing that you are a plant or flora empath what is it you can do with your gifts? Well, the obvious things are to have a house full of plants and a yard full of the garden. Plants can bring many benefits to your home and you can then hear them and give them what they need. You can nurture them, and they can do the same for you. Plants will change the energy of your home, improve the air and make your home look better just by their presence.

Have as big a garden as you can possibly manage. You can become a professional landscaper, a florist, a farmer, or even a master gardener. You can grow fruits and vegetables for people who have none, and work at a community garden as a volunteer.

Earth Empath

This empath is perhaps the most unusual of all. Imagine being in touch with the earth in such a way that you can "feel" a volcano before it erupts or "know" a tornado is in the area before the weather service does. This is the life of the earth empath. In touch with the soul of the earth and all its trauma and pain. You can feel the earth's energy. In today's environment of climate change, it must be very intense energy. On the other hand, the earth empath is able to warn people of coming disasters with the weather. You can be energized by a beautiful day, a rainbow, a waterfall. You can be devasted by the dying coral in the ocean or the wildlife covered in oil from an ocean spill. You feel the love the sun and moon have for the earth as they care for it.

You are nourished by the richness of the earth, her plants, and her flowers. You can feel the awesome power of a hurricane or a thunderstorm. You feel whatever happens to the earth in your body. You know when the weather is going to change before it does change. You find peace in the Grand Canyon's awesome beauty and the Badlands desolate quiet. You'd rather go camping than stay at a 4-star hotel. You'd rather lay outside and commune with the stars than go to a party or a bar.

You feel the love of mother earth all the time. Yet you cannot withstand the pain at what humans do to her and how much she hurts. It is the human-made disasters that hurt the most. Tornadoes, hurricanes, floods are all devastating, but much, much worse are the oil spills, the air pollution, the carbon emissions. These are much more painful for the earth empath because they don't have to be. For the earth empaths, there is depression and anxiety with any unrest in the earth's life force. When that happens the earth empath should take a walk, go to the beach or the mountains. Commune with the stars.

Talk to the earth. Find out how things are going for her. Stay open to anything she may say, anything you feel, hear or see. So how should you channel this energy? Many earth empaths understand and share with indigenous traditions and people the medicine of the earth. Nature heals and the earth empaths are able to tap into that healing energy.

You can be a healer. You can be an environmentalist. You can be a fighter for mother earth and against the causes of climate change. You can be a marine biologist and fight to save the oceans. There is an unlimited number of pathways for an earth empath. Volunteer to do conservation work as a preservationist. You can become an educator in conservation and preservation or lecture about the coming changes in the climate. You can help others to deal with the pain that mother earth goes through.

On a smaller scale, you can intuit where the earth needs the most help, where her energy is blocked and try to help there. Improve your personal space through energy work such as Feng Shui. You can try to heal these places with your own earth healing energy.

No, you can't stop a hurricane. You can't stop a volcano. But you can move the energy a little. You can heal a part of the earth by doing what you can do. Send out the white energy to the places where you feel the earth's energy is stuck. Like you made a bubble around yourself to shield yourself from too much of other's energy, now you can send out a bubble of light to encase the hurting piece of earth that you can help. It is hard to be an earth empath, but you must do what you can.

Last but certainly not least spend all the time you can with mother nature. Listen to her. Feel her heartbeat in the earth, the trees. Visit the redwoods and sequoia trees and let your awe and love permeate their beings. Be grateful for all the earth has given us. Just being with her will send her healing energy.

The Unusual Empaths

You can see that these three types of empaths are unusual. They are not ordinary – if there is any ordinary – empath. These empaths deal with everything any other empath deals with. But for them, there is even more. For the animal and plant, the empath is a joyous loving more, most of the time, but it is still overwhelming and painful when the animals and plants are in pain. The earth empath may exult in the most glorious things about the earth and then agonize over her pain and destruction.

There are many kinds of empaths as we have seen. These are three very special ones.

10 CHAPTER 10

Can Animals be Empaths?

Ask anyone who lives with a dog. Ask anyone who has a companion animal. Ask Jane Goodall or Dianne Fosse. Can animals be empaths? The answer will be a resounding YES! The answer will be anecdotal of course. Still, the answer will be a resounding YES! It is almost impossible to live with social, pack animals and not see how empathetic they can be, but are they empaths? What does the science say? Does science even care or is all the evidence in either direction anecdotal?

We will start with science and we will end with the tales of those who live most closely with animals. I believe not only can they be empaths – it is undeniable to me that they are natural empaths, without a lot of the boundaries that human beings have. But we will get to that. First the science.

Current Research Results

There is no need to spend time going over again what an empath is or what has gone into scientific studies of humans as empaths. However, let's just refresh our minds that there are emotional and cognitive empathic systems. The empath deals with both behavioral matching and physiological matching. The interactions between emotional and cognitive perspectives are complex and intense. Early studies did not distinguish the responses of animals that would be cognitive or emotional – how they responded to the observer and how they responded to the "other". It was felt without this; animals could not be considered empathic.

However, just as perspectives of empathic abilities in people have changed, so too has our entire perception of animals and what they are capable of. Those that live with humans are constantly in the position of exposure to the pain, grief or distress of "their people". Most of their people would attest to their companion animal expressing empathy in those situations. Some more than others and dogs more than cats, but the experience of empathy is there.

In these situations, from a controlled scientific point of view however, it is not always clear how emotionally involved the animal is. There is clearly interest on the part of the animal but is there really an emotional as well as a cognitive response? New studies are beginning to look at this question in different ways in an attempt to really answer the questions.

To be an empath you must feel what others feel. You must also feel that feeling within yourself. We know that humans can do this, but can your cat actually feel what you feel? Can your dog? We empathize with our dog, but can our dog empathize with us? Scientists and veterinary researchers are beginning to believe that they can.

However, they would tell you that your dog is more likely to be empathetic than your cat. Why? Biologists think that it is more likely that social animals – pack animals – like your dog will be empathetic. It is more likely that elephants, primates, rats, wolves, and even chickens are empathic. But maybe not your cat. Still, if you live with cats you believe they empathize with you when you are down, and they come to lay on you and "comfort" you. Still, the official line at this point is if you are in a social group, and you are continuing to evolve than you are likely to feel the pain of the other members of your group.

Originally empathic behavior was thought by science and biology experts to be a strictly human activity. However recent studies have given us new evidence that many non-human species are capable of emotional empathy. Two studies were done with chickens. The first study used a group of chicks and their mothers. The mothers were made to believe the chicks were endangered and they did respond. In the second group, the control chicken and the observers were not related in any way. In this group, the observers did not show any concern for the control individual.

This does leave us with the possibility that an empathic response is only possible with chickens when they belong with a group and not an unknown individual. It might also have to do with the relationship between the control and the observers. Either way, it was clear that the first group of adults watching the distress of their chicks did indeed appear to have an empathic response.

The only other study involved Jane Goodall and Chimpan-Zeez from 1986, 1990 and De Waal in 1982 and 1989. The goal of these studies was to show that chimps could display empathy and what type. They also looked for what type of behavior would be needed to instigate empathy from the chimps. The true goal was to show enough to spur on furthermore rigorous studies. There were six chimps involved in this study and Goodall had examples of empathic behavior.

There are also a lot of species that have emotional epicenters in their brains that are very much like ours. It is actually possible that the non-human species are capable of a far wider range of emotions than humans. They also have a larger capacity for empathy with a larger neocortex.

- Anecdotal Evidence

Elephants mourn and even have funerals. Yet geese flying in formation will not leave a lost or injured goose behind alone. They will leave one goose to stay with the injured one as long as that one is alive. Penguins and coyotes' mate for life and there have been many stories about dolphins, birds, and whales. We now know that all these animals have what we would call consciousness – they know themselves when they see their reflection in the mirror. As previously mentioned, they are capable of a wide range of emotions and they mourn their dead. It appears that dogs can do all of this except recognizing themselves in a mirror.

In his book, Beyond Words: How Animals Think and Feel, by Carl Safina, says when it comes to animals' intelligence, we are asking the wrong questions. This comes from being human-centric and having little respect for all other animals. Instead of wondering how animals are in and of themselves, our sciences ask how are animals like us? In his very moving book, Safina asks the right questions about elephants in Kenya and wolves in Canada. Safina makes the case for animal intelligence and empathy far beyond any current thinking.

" Ever since Descartes denied the sentience of other beings, objective empiricism insisted that we resist anthropomorphism so devotedly that science has ignored what is most obvious; animals think, feel, love, grieve, mourn, celebrate, play, and suffer, not as we do, but more importantly, in their own way. They are individuals with personalities just as humans are individuals with personalities.

Safina points to our sharp scientific division between human brains and other brains as our great hubristic folly. He explains that just as we are closely related to animals physically, we can also assume we are related to them mentally. We are conscious by virtue of the same complex processes, and we are all, as he puts it, on one vast "continuum." He elaborates on how closely related we are to other animals; that our sentience is part of that continuous family of diverse forms of sentience."
- Julie Morley Amazon reviewer -

With this book, Safina has broken all the rules and all the stereotypes about animals. He has come to believe that all animals are sentient, intelligent and capable of empathy. He is only one person working with anecdotal data. Yet his premise and conclusions have sparked animals feel empathy. They feel empathy for their own families, species, other animals and of course us.

Therapy Animals

An exceptional example of animals, especially dogs, exhibiting empathy is the therapy animal. This too is anecdotal. This too is information gleaned from stories. Wonderful stories about how therapy dogs seem to know just which patient in the hospital needs them the most. Which room should they go to without their handler taking them? Here are a few of their stories.

The cat – was known to be so in touch with the people he cared for that he knew when someone was going to die. He was known to go to the room of a patient, curl up on the bed with them and stay there until the patient passed on. He would then leave the room and move on to the next terminally ill patient.

The pig – works with a speech pathologist and special needs children, mostly those with autism. He is so good at his job that a child with autism who had never spoken talked to the therapy pig.

The corgi – she was a shy dog, a rescue, but her person worked with adults with developmental disabilities. This corgi was not a trained therapy animal, but she was filled with empathy for these people. When she would visit the center, she would let anyone pet her, pound on her head, hug her tightly. These were things not even her family could do with her at home.

The pit bull – because he was a pit bull rescue his early life had been a nightmare of pain and abuse. He understood what it was to hurt, to feel scared, alone, abandoned. He works in a long-term care unit now and comforts those who have no family or friends, those in pain and scared of death. He climbs right up next to them and is as gentle as he can be with old and brittle people. He lays his head on their chest if possible and just stays there for a while. He has no handler. He just moves from room to room seeing who needs his help.

Companion Animals

Try telling anyone who lives with an animal that they are not capable of emotions and empathy. These days most will laugh at the suggestion. They know that when they are down and their dog comes and puts his head on their knee, the dog is expressing empathy, that the dog is feeling his person's pain. Every dog owner has experienced those moments of thinking that his dog knows exactly how he is feeling and wants to help him.

Is your dog really in touch with your feelings? Does he feel what you feel? Is he an empath? If he is not and you are hiding your pain, how does he know that you are upset? Why does your dog choose to cuddle or express her affection at just that moment when you are feeling most down?

Many psychologists, biologists, and animal behaviorists still don't believe this is empathy. That is because they believe that dogs' emotional life is like that of a two-year-old. Their explanation for this behavior is that the dog is picking up on your feelings without having any understanding of them and without feeling them within his own body as the human empath does. They believe that your dog becomes upset because you are upset. He is seeking his own comfort when he lays his head in your lap or licks your tears.

Yet we have seen that researchers now know that the non-human neocortex is larger than our own and animals may be capable of far greater empathy than humans. The culture is slowly changing with animals just as it has with humans. There is much great understanding and acceptance of their intelligence and capacity for emotional empathy. At this point, we still really have no absolute answer either way.

We have seen our companion dogs' express sorrow and grief when a friend dies – human or animal. We have seen them in what appears to be the act of comforting each other. More and more science, animal behaviorist, and veterinarians are all moving in the direction of believing that animals do indeed have a wide array of emotional capacity and can certainly have the same empathic energy as humans.

More Anecdotal Evidence

Here are a few more real-life stories that indicate that animals are smarter, more emotional, more compassionate and more empathic than humans ever thought they were.

- Many people are terrified of rodents and especially rats. They have been portrayed as dirty, disease-carrying, frightening and vicious animals. Yet this does not appear to be their character in real life at all. They are stereotypes for dishonest or criminal people who we call "rats" or "You dirty rat". Yet the real animal just might be one of the most compassionate on earth.

Lab rats have often been found to choose pain for themselves over pain for another rat when they understood the situation. Rats in one study were taught that if they pulled the lever in front of them, they were rewarded with chocolate. Then they were taught that if they pulled the lever, another rat would almost drown. Almost all of the rats in the experiment refused to pull the lever. Their fellow rats were more important to them than the reward.

- When conservationist, Lawrence Anthony, died from a heart attack after years of working with African Elephants, two herds of elephants somehow knew, and they walked 12 hours to his house to mourn for him. They acted just as they would act if an elephant from one of their own herds had died. They stayed at his house mourning him for two full days, then made the trip back to their home.

- There was a chimp at Central Washington University who could speak in sign language. His caretaker Kat was pregnant and suddenly absent from him for a few weeks. The chimp was very upset about her being gone and no one had told him why. He was angry with Kat when she came back until she signed an apology and told him her baby had died. He looked at her silently for a long time and then he signed "cry" and ran his finger down her face.

- In an African country several years ago there was a gang of men beating and raping little girls. They had a 12-year-old and were

93

trying to force her to get married to one of them. Suddenly a pride of lions appeared and attacked the gang, chasing them away. They then laid down with the girl for over 12 hours so the gang would not come back. The girl's family finally came to find her, and they were shocked and frightened by the lions. But the pride simply got up and walked away, leaving her to her family as they went home to theirs.

With mostly anecdotal evidence it can be seen that animals certainly appear to have developed emotions and empathic behavior. Now science is beginning to catch up with what so many animal "people" have always known. Yes, animals can be empaths and they probably are.

Questions remain, however, if animals really are empaths do, they face the same concerns and issues as human empaths do? How do they protect themselves from emotional overload? Is it because they share all these emotions and empathic experiences with each other in ways that humans do not? Do they have coping mechanisms that we are unaware of? Could they teach humans to share the empathic burden more and bring more joy into the world?

Unanswered questions that may or may not have an answer some day. The more humans admit that animals are sentient, have lives, loves, joys and sorrows just as we do, the more answers we will find.

11 CHAPTER 11

Celebrating your Gift

We have covered a lot of ground in these previous nine chapters. We have learned about taking care of our empathic children and helping them grow up with protections in place for emotional overload. We have learned how to take care of our empathic selves and how to heal those whose pain we feel. What we have not done is celebrate what it means to live as a healthy, balanced empath. We have not celebrated this gift we were born with and have nurtured to this point.

For many being an empath is more burden than celebration and we recognize this and have attempted to honor it with ways of making it better. Yet for many others being an empath is not a burden but a joy. It is for many a reason to celebrate. It is for many a gift that enlightens their lives, their path and they understand that it is a valuable gift. It is a gift that adds to their own value.

It is this we wish to celebrate as we close this book. You are worth celebrating. You are not alone. You are a gift to the world. You have much to give to the world. You have learned that there is nothing wrong with you. Rather there is something quite right with you. What is very right about you is your empathic capacity to change the world.

Yes, it can be tough. It can be overwhelming to feel the pain of everyone else as well as your own. Yet this gift allows you to experience life and to experience the world in ways that those not in touch with their empathic energy cannot. They can imagine what you feel. You can feel what they feel. This gives you insight and grace that you would not otherwise have. It more often than not leads to compassion, tolerance, understanding, and love.

Why is your empathic ability and energy a gift?

- All of your senses are heightened. You smell more, hear more, taste more. Just imagine how mundane life might be if your flowers didn't smell the way you smell them if your food did not have an extra level of flavor because your capacity to taste is greater. Now imagine if everyone could experience their physical senses at the level that you do. You might even get to the point of smelling disease in people and helping them to get treatment before it is too late.
- You are a natural born healer. This is the essence of your empathetic gift. You know when emotional healing is needed even if the other person does not know they need it. Whether you

use your hands, a musical instrument, your voice or another tool, you are a healer of energy and you can learn to help more and more people throughout your life.

- You are more aware, more in touch with your deepest self, with your non-physical senses as well as your physical ones. You may sense danger before it comes and be able to do something to keep it from coming.

- With the depth of feeling, you are capable of you can live at a much greater level of intensity and enthusiasm and joy than others who are not as in touch with their deepest feelings. You can be more compassionate, more understanding, kinder...

- You probably see things a little differently than non-empaths and think just a little differently than non-empaths. You are creative in so many ways because you are so close to the essence of life. Yes, that's right. With your capacity for feeling, loving, being... you are closer to the truth of what life is about than those who are not empathic. You are more self-aware and yes you need solitude and quiet at times. But that too is part of the gift to renew your energy, your life.

- You understand what the other person needs and the cost of not getting what they need. Therefore you have the ability to try to help them get what they need even if they don't know that they need it.

- You can read non-verbal cues and pick up on others needs when most others can't. You might be the only person in the room who can help that person in need. You might be the only person who even knows there is a need.

- You can pick up on the needs of those who cannot speak for themselves. For instance, the earth, the animals, plants, humans without the capacity to speak. More and more these gifts are accepted into our culture such as with Animal Empaths or Communicators who speak the telepathic language of the animals and can translate it back for us.

- You can't lie to an empath. We will know it every time. Too often in our culture, a person who is broken inside will tell you they are fine. You know they are not. You can help them. You can let them know that you know, and you are there to support them.

- When someone tries to lie for evil purposes or to hide something, you will know. You can't be fooled very often, and you know when someone is playing with your head.

- This is all a gift, not a curse. You are more in charge than you feel and more in charge than non-empaths will ever be. You have an understanding that surpasses anything they can feel. You can even help them to develop this wonderful gift for themselves.

Like most empaths, it has not always been clear to you that this was a gift to be celebrated. As you look at all these reasons why it is a gift the only response can be to celebrate it, to celebrate life. In this world at this time there is a lot of fear, pain, confusion, and yes evil. You feel it all and there is also a lot of joy, excitement, clarity of purpose and love, love, love. You feel it all.

Often what you feel is not yours at all and you may have spent years figuring that out. But now you know it is not yours and you can let it go.

Just set those feelings free out into the universe as they are not yours and they are not attached to anyone else either. Just send them away.

You can learn to manage your energy. You can learn to shield yourself and in so doing you can learn to be more and more, the essence of love which is all we really want to be.

As society changes more and more you will feel supported and you will see how you are not alone. You can be a part of making those changes happen. It seems that the medical field and of course the mental health field may be the ones to lead the way to this new and openly empathic society.

What if you could imagine a society in which your empathic gift could be your career? That society is being built today. The Cleveland Clinic even has a Chief Empathy Officer on staff – another kind of CEO. Let's celebrate it! Let's make a difference in the world.

But what is a Chief Empathy Officer? Is it a new staff position with new responsibilities or just a cute change to the Chief Executive Officer without any real change in the environment or culture of the company?

At the Cleveland Clinic, it is neither of those. It is the Chief Executive Officer, but it is more than lip service to empathy. They also have a Chief Experience Officer. At the Cleveland Clinic, they seem to have learned that in medicine empathy is the key to everything. They take that key very seriously as well.

They have empathy training for the staff and the caregivers, including how the caregivers treat each other and not just the patients. Do they have empathy for each other and how do they cultivate that. It is the caregivers who are often on the receiving end of the patient's frustration or the families impatient. They talk with patients for hours and those conversations can be very emotional and take a toll on the staff.

That's where empathy comes in and at the Cleveland Clinic, it is from the top down. The training is much more than the traditional say this not that and show a bunch of slides on how to behave with the patients and each other. No, what is new at the Cleveland Clinic is how seriously they are about this and how they actually model the behavior in very concrete ways. So when a nurse leaves this training she knows in her own body and emotions what it is like to be a patient or a caregiver who is valued and is not invisible.

The goal is for a holistic patient experience while maintaining the respect and dignity of the staff who is responsible for that experience. If your staff has to work three consecutive shifts because of call-ins, then you don't respect your staff enough or have empathy enough to have an additional staff or per diems able to fill in. An exhausted caregiver isn't likely to have much empathy for the patient or for the staff member who just came on after having 8 hours off. This is what they are attempting to accomplish at the Cleveland Clinic with a Chief Empathy Officer and a Chief Experience Office. The right technology can be a part of the solution, but without a move toward full facility empathy, technology won't change much.

More and more companies of all sorts are turning to empathy to turn their organizations into the best they can be. More companies have CEOs that are really Chief Empathy Officers. That title means different things at different companies and as we just saw, Cleveland Clinic even has a Chief Experience Office.

What really is the role of empathy in business these days? Hasn't it always been about the customer, the end user, the client? Where does empathy make it better? Empathy is about knowing where that customer is coming from and where they want to end up. It's not even about what a customer needs to do because these days they do what they want to do. Empathy is wrapping our heads and our hands around that "want" and then designing our products or systems to deliver on it.

The Chief Empathy Officer is there to create an empathic link between the company and the customer so you will know exactly what they want and also be able to move them toward what you deliver. It is so important for the CEO to embrace the idea of empathy as a guiding force in their company. Many do not.

Empathy matters and empathy from the top matters more. People have many choices today and consciously or unconsciously, employees, customers, investors even vendors will gravitate to empathic companies. This has its roots in the scientific studies we mentioned in chapter 3. The more a company offers what a client needs instead of what a client wants, the more stress is created in the client and the more elevated levels of cortisol take over in his body.

Cortisol is a hormone that when elevated causes confused thinking and emotional reacting. This happens when your supplier offers you something you don't want and insists it is best for your business. Without empathy, many companies treat their customers this way. These days customers push back. You will get more with an attitude of empathy than with this attitude.

When empathy runs your company, your customers and your staff relax, cortisol reduces, and dopamine and oxytocin kick in to reduce cortisol even more. Now you have your customer in your state of empathy and read to buy what you have to offer.

The problem is too many CEOs don't want to be Chief Empathy Officer. They see it as giving up their hard-earned power. However once they see the difference operating out of empathy can bring, the less resistance there will be. Can you imagine a worldwide community of CEO's operating out of empathy?

Most CEO's are afraid of losing control while they still hold all the accountability for the company's success. If they think empathy will cost them control, they won't do it no matter how good it seems. The challenge for the board and perhaps a Chief Empathy Officer is to sell the CEO on the reasons to make an empathetic culture?

No matter what you do you have to make sure everyone involved get into the last time this happened.

We know as empaths that rejection and hate will not solve any of the problems the world faces today. Only love, only compassion, only understanding, and only empathy will be able to do that. We have to overcome but with empathy as our guide, we can do it. Use your empathic energy for good. When you do it will make it a little less burdensome and a little more celebratory.

Some Additional Thoughts on Living as an Empath

It's not easy but it's glorious. It will drain you completely and it will fill you up more than you can imagine. Let it be a gift that you celebrate and not a burden that you carry. Find a mentor to help you on your path.

 Spending time with an experienced mentor could be one of the best things you can do for yourself. A mentor has probably experienced anything you are going to experience and can support you through it. Take advantage of the many books, courses, audio tools available to empaths. Most of all is with your people. Find empath groups to support you.

Celebrate your empathic abilities and energy. I have seen many places where empaths say that their empathic energy is their superpower. In the age of few heroes, maybe it would be good to have a superpower. We have these gifts for the good of all the earth and not just ourselves or our species. Your empathic energy allows you to be kind in an often-unkind world. You can be compassionate and make life better today for one other person. Yes, it can be a superpower and you can be a hero. Celebrate it.

As you celebrate your empathic self, don't forget to follow your dreams. You can change the world and follow your dreams at the same time. So many empaths neglect themselves, forget to feed their own souls and forget to even dream. Don't follow them. Follow your heart. You are a spiritual being with your own purpose in life. Find it an follow it. Celebrate it.

Surround yourself with inspiring people. When an empath is with inspiring people the empath is inspired by the energy and excitement he picks up. Yes, you want to help those who are down, but you need to refresh yourself first in order to do so. Surrounding yourself with inspiring people, going to hear talks by inspiring people, listening to podcasts of things like the TED Talks, will leave you inspired, with more to give and more to celebrate.

Make time for yourself and make time to celebrate. Make following your dreams your sacred duty. Choose for yourself how you will spend your time, your empathic energy, your life. Don't let others choose for you. Just because you have empathic energy doesn't mean you have to give all your life energy away. Fulfill your own sacred calling and celebrate it! Celebrate yourself!

CONCLUSION

We seem to have reached the end of the journey. We set out to learn about empaths. Who are they? Where do they come from? What do they do? What do they need?

In Chapter one we learned what an empath is. That person who takes in everything others gives out in terms of feelings. That special person who knows what you are feeling, and you never told them. You never showed them. In fact, you might not have even known yourself what you were really feeling. But they did. The empath knew. She just knew.

But where did that knowledge come from and was it real or just imaginative? Was it truly extra senses or was it a scam? There are no real psychics are there? Chapter two showed us just how old the existence of empaths in society was. It also showed us the history or empaths – who were they? Who believed them? Who named them?

Some of those questions were answered in the next two chapters on Nature or Nurture and the place of empaths in the mind of the scientific community. We learned that the existence of the empath is the result of both nature and nurture. We all have the capacity to be active empaths, but some people were born to open to it and just "being" it. While many others know it is there and set out to learn about it, to train themselves to use the gifts of an empath.

You also learned that there are many kinds of empaths – those whose gifts are primarily vision, or hearing, or smell. Those who can feel the feelings of animals, plants, nature. Those who can sense the future or know what is going on in someone's body so they can heal it. The diversity is great and something to celebrate.

We saw how science has moved from skepticism to acknowledgment and even proof that something is happening in our brains when we are experiencing the feelings of others. Those feelings of others become our own and the neural pathways in our brain show it happening. With this knowledge in hand, society is moving toward openness and acceptance of the empathic gift that is desperately needed by struggling empaths.

Empaths can often feel alone, maybe even think they are going crazy. They have all these feelings that they don't know what to do with or where they came from. Now those empaths can be helped by a scientific community, a neurobiological community and a mental health community that knows what the empath is experiencing is real and natural. You don't have to feel crazy anymore.

In fact, you can now support your children or any children you know who are growing up as acknowledged empaths. They are open and they are often overwhelmed. They need to know they are normal. They need acceptance and to know that they are not crazy. Half their feelings don't belong to them. It can be very scary and confusing. Now you have the scientific knowledge you need to help them grow up healthy and whole. You even know famous empaths you can tell them about and cool quotes about empaths.

You learned in chapters 5 and 7 what the potential of an empath is, what you can do with your gift and tools you can use to heal others and protect yourself. You even learned about creating a bubble shield around yourself when it all gets to be too much. You have tools in your kit now and you know how to use them.

You learned to keep yourself safe in many different ways. You could cloak yourself in that bubble shield or any other kind of shield you want to invent. You can use meditation and prayer to stay centered and focused. In fact, meditation and mindfulness go hand in hand with empathic energy. They are almost survival skills for an active empath. So it is very important to learn to meditate. Journaling and/or seeing a counselor are also very good tools for keeping yourself grounded, sane and safe when all the emotions of the world start flying in at you at once.

Chapter nine took a turn in another direction entirely and a little out of the ordinary. Is your dog empathic? Most of us think so but the verdict is still out as far as the scientific community is concerned. There are a few studies but there need to be a lot more. There needs to be a change in how the scientific community views animals and shares those views with us. This change is in the works but it may be slow. The less research there is into animal communication, feelings, emotions, and intelligence the slower the process will be. We encourage more studies in this area to show that animals are sentient, with emotions and more smarts than we have ever given them credit for.

Therapy animals, companion animals, and some very special animals' stories all seem to indicate that they are more intelligent, more empathic, more much more of everything than humans have credited them with. Just ask your dog. She'll tell you how smart she is.

Finally, we called for a celebration. We called for a celebration of gifts of the empath. We were delighted to find that the Cleveland Clinic has a

Chief Empathy Officer. We hope it's a sign of the future and it seems logical that it should be the medical community, the healing arts, that embrace the energy of the empath before so much else of our society does.

I hope this has been educational and inspirational. If you are an active empath celebrate it! Celebrate all that life offers you to see, smell. Taste, hear and feel. Celebrate yourself and remember that empathy is a gift. Let it keep giving to you and from you. For with an open active empathy we can change the world for the better.

FINAL WORDS

We seem to have reached the end of the journey. So did we accomplish that which we set out to do? Did we cover all the bases? Are you convinced that being an empath is simply a part of being a human being? It is an essential part, a different part, but just a part of being human. We were all born with the potential and it can be taught to each of us. We can learn to develop our own empathic abilities.

There is a myriad of people involved today in building a more empathetic society, a more compassionate world and they can be found in any and every profession. The Center for Building a Culture of Empathy is at the forefront of this movement. At their webpage, you will find a list of some of those myriads of people working to build such a culture.

They are scientists, doctors, biologists, neurologists, businesspeople, medical personnel, healers in their own right, researchers, psychologists, psychiatrists, sociologists, anthropologists, authors, entrepreneurs, life coaches, self-help experts, professors, childhood development experts, the Center for Nonviolent Communication, teachers, trainers, and many, many more. Thousands and hundreds of thousands of empaths.

The culture is definitely changing for the better for the active empath. But that means it is also changing for the better for everyone else as well. For if we take our empathic gifts joyfully out into the world and walk in everyone else's shoes, we will make the world a better place. Empaths can change the world with their understanding, compassion, tolerance, and respect for what everyone else is living through.

We talk so little about the joys of empathy and so much about the struggle. When you are in a roomful of happy, healthy people how do you feel? Would you choose to give away your empathic energy now? If you knew that you could be a part of spreading that kind of joy around the world, to your family and friends, to anyone who stepped into your life, would that not have the same if not more valuable than the work with those who are in pain?

Could you change those who are in pain into those who share the joy of life? Could that be the sacred calling of the empath and how we can change the world we live in? Could it be we are meant to feel this joy at such a deep, intense level that we understand it is this kind of joy and love that can change the world? This joy can heal those in pain.

So often these days you see a poster, a message about all those people who are not "ok", but because their disease is not readily visible or their mental illness doesn't "show", everyone around them thinks they are just fine. They may be dying inside, in terrible physical or emotional pain and yet they are alone with it unless they bring it up.

When the world is full of compassionate, active empaths those people will no longer be alone. They will no longer be invisible. We see them. We feel them. We can be there for them and support them in any way they would want to be supported. This is how we change the world. This is how we build empathy in everyone. This is the challenge and the reward of being an empath.

CPSIA information can be obtained
at www.ICGtesting.com
Printed in the USA
BVHW090830240521
607631BV00013B/360